F. Taverner Graham

Reasonable Elocution

A text-book for schools, colleges, clergymen, lawyers, actors, etc

F. Taverner Graham

Reasonable Elocution

A text-book for schools, colleges, clergymen, lawyers, actors, etc

ISBN/EAN: 9783337233150

Printed in Europe, USA, Canada, Australia, Japan

Cover: Foto ©Paul-Georg Meister /pixelio.de

More available books at **www.hansebooks.com**

Reasonable Elocution.

A

TEXT-BOOK

FOR

SCHOOLS, COLLEGES, CLERGYMEN, LAWYERS, ACTORS, Etc.

BY

Mrs. F. TAVERNER GRAHAM.

―――――――――

A. S. BARNES AND COMPANY,
NEW YORK AND CHICAGO.

Entered according to Act of Congress, in the year 1874, by

A. S. BARNES & CO.,

In the Office of the Librarian of Congress, at Washington.

INTRODUCTION.

THAT the Art of Reading will "come naturally" is a common fallacy, with which we almost constantly delude ourselves. Even if it were true, it would offer little encouragement to those who appreciate the beauty and importance of the art; for some method of reading is always taught, and as this is extremely likely to be radically wrong, all chance of attaining a strictly natural style of reading is destroyed at an early period of the pupil's career by errors of instruction and the contagion of bad example.

In point of fact, however, Elocution is both a science and an art—resting on positive laws, founded in the nature of things; and, as in the case of any other art or science, these laws never come by nature, but must be mastered by study and practice. The master must have spent hours and days in careful research and patient delineation of the most insignificant natural points; he must have familiarized himself with all science that bears even remotely on his art; otherwise he exposes himself to the danger of introducing incongruities into his work, and of committing blunders, which will be apparent at once to the trained observer. Sculptors, for instance, are obliged to study anatomy, in order to avoid the mistakes they would perpetrate were they ignorant of the distribution of the bones and muscles, their movements and attachments in the human frame. But even this is not enough; if the sculptor be unfamiliar with the theory of "equilibrium," he may spoil his work by representing the perpendicular from the centre of gravity as falling unnaturally. And the necessity for scientific knowledge in the painter is even more evident; it is the disregard of linear, and the lack of all aerial perspective, that constitutes the absurdity of Chinese pictures; yet perspective rests on strictly natural laws which science alone can interpret.

The artistic effects produced by an elocutionist, an orator, or an actor, represent purely objective and subjective phenomena; and they can be true representations only in so far as they conform to the natural laws of these phenomena. Before they can thus conform, the delineator of human feelings and passions must understand *what* are the laws and under what conditions they vary. For this reason, the study of psychology is of the utmost importance to the elocutionist; it will enable him to indicate by his inflections of voice, by intonation and by emphasis, his mental attitude toward certain thoughts and sentiments without digression to explain it; and this is nearly the whole art of Elocution.

Every clergyman, orator, and actor, possesses at least a stock of empirical generalizations which guide him in his exposition of the matter in hand; but to have a general idea only of what we are to do and of how we are to express ourselves under given circumstances, is not sufficient; such meagre knowledge will not enable us to delineate different shades of thought or various and complex emotions. It is this sort of vague impression—or rather, quite definite ignorance—that gives us that large class of persons who render all its passions with extreme violence, and after exhausting themselves (and their audience) imagine that they have done all that "elocution" can do. These persons are not confined to the stage; we have them in the pulpit, at the bar, in Congress, on the rostrum. They of the pulpit will declaim on the attributes of the Almighty, or the happiness of those who have found that peace which the Saviour promised, in as forcible tones, as fast "time," and with as energetic gesticulations, as they employ in denunciations of the sinner, or in depicting the sufferings of the lost. The lawyer who affects this style of delivery will throw as much emphasis into a description of the clothes his client wore on the night of the assault as into his execration of the assailant's villainy. And there is another description of public speaker, who has a fine voice, and who employs his full deep tones alike on all he utters,—the deepest emotions, the simplest narrative, the most violent passions. He has a particular fondness for the "semitone," that plaintive minor key, symbolical of grief or melancholy. He reads the psalms of praise with the sad half tones that belong to penitence; making the voluntary and joyful offering of thanksgiving a lugubrious task which he feels very melancholy (for so his tone indicates) in performing. He uses emotional tones on sentences or sentiments that indicate emotion in no degree; or if he employs tones which have a natural relation to the ideas expressed, his reading will as frequently verge on the burlesque as on the grand; for "burlesque" is simply an inversion of natural laws—as when trivial or absurd sentiments are delivered in heroic tones and with impressive emphasis. When little or no emotion exists in idea, tones that are full and sonorous should be used but sparingly, or not at all; as feeling rises they may be employed more freely, and only in their intensity where the climax of passion is reached.

Many people object to any special study of elocution for the reason that they do not expect to become professional readers or public speakers. Would they object to the study of literature because they cannot hope to become authors? Or to that of music because they would never dream of becoming a Beethoven, Mozart, or Gluck? Or to that of astronomy or any of the sciences because they can never aspire to the position of a Herschel or a Humboldt? Who most keenly enjoys a fine picture? Certainly he who has the most extended knowledge of what the picture represents—of those facts in nature or in life which he finds delineated therein, and on the accuracy of which he can pronounce. Why is it that the person of cultivated mind takes so much more pleasure in a noble poem than does one who is ignorant? Is it not because a wider acquaintance with the subject, and the ability to compare its beauties with those charms similar, and yet different, possessed by other poems, causes him to see in the work many things of which the uneducated one is ignorant? So with elocution. A knowledge of it not only enables us to interpret thought and emotions to others, but assists us very greatly in understanding them ourselves. The person who can read well is, even as a listener, very different from him who can not.

Still another fallacy, far too current even among intelligent people, is the idea that those who display the higher elocutionary accomplishments possess a "genius" which it would be vain to endeavor to acquire—the cultivation of which is beyond the reach of art. Such ideas are born of ignorance; for so thinks the savage of the simplest computation in arithmetic, or the untutored boor of the wonders of the magic lantern. A thorough knowledge of the principles of any art will enable a determined student to approach perfection in it. If he possesses these principles in elocution, he may on them found his own style of reading or speaking, which may be natural and excellent, and yet very different from his neighbor's founded on the same principle.

The more important of these principles I shall endeavor to make plain in the following chapters. It will be observed that I do this rather by examples, and exercises, and illustrations, than by exposition. To the mere reader this will perhaps seem cumbrous, and even perplexing; but teachers will understand full well that it is the only efficient method of impressing new facts on the minds of the young, or of converting theoretical into practical knowledge.

F. T. G.

ABSTRACT OF CONTENTS.

IN this little work I have endeavored to supply to teachers, their pupils, and other persons, a long-felt need of an Elocutionary Text-book, founded on philosophical principles. Principals of schools and others have frequently said to me, "Why do you not publish a book which shall embrace the principles you teach, and various exercises illustrative of those principles?" I decided that a brief work, with the natural laws of Time, Tone, and Emphasis explained, and their *truth* proved, would answer the general purpose better than the sort of book I had at first contemplated writing. The first division in "Reasonable Elocution" explains the necessity for, and the ease with which the speaking and reading voice can be cultivated; the manner of so doing, and exercises for the purpose; the plan being very similar to that used for the singing voice, the difference being that sentences are used for scales instead of "sea" or "do, re, mi," etc., and that they are spoken on regularly ascending and descending scales, designed for increasing the flexibility and compass of the speaking voice. Exercises for distinct utterance are also included in this division.

The division on "*Time*" is explanatory of the mental valuation of thoughts and sentiments by the changes in the "Time" of rendering. The natural management of parentheses, similes, quotations, metaphors, the marvelous, parables, etc., is through changes in *Time;* the philosophy of the principle which governs these changes, and their propriety proved. Illustrations of the different principles.

EMPHASIS.

Its philosophy, and practical execution. Errors in emphasis common among scholars. Natural laws which should guide us in emphasis.

The "Emphatic Clause" is a *new* fact or idea, now presented for the first time—it should be ascertained without additional particular. The "Unemphatic Clause" presents *no* new idea; it may be of repetition, of sequence, of anticipation, etc., etc. Examples.

Emphatic Word. When the root idea is a *word*, that word is emphatic. Emphasis, by "*massing*" several words, presenting one and the same idea. Examples.

Clauses unemphatic through having been mentally projected. Examples.

Emphasis by transfer when there are repeated words. Examples.

A repeated word, having a new signification, has all the logical power of a new word. Examples.

Psychological positives and negatives. Inflections of voice indicate positive or negative attitudes of mind with regard to thoughts. The mental stand-point, from which we regard certain ideas or sentiments, gathered by auditors from the sort of inflections we employ. The *main* purpose of the speaker should be indicated by true inflections. Examples.

Lectures, sermons, etc., are rendered obscure and

fused through inattention to this obvious law of nature. Examples from the parables, etc.

The "*wave*" of the voice, ⌣ ⌢ ⌣ ⌢, or vacillating inflection, mark the episode, the illustration; they indicate a departure from the main track of thought. They are produced through the mind's vacillating between the illustration and the subject illustrated; the return to the main thought is naturally marked by a return to the usual upward ╱ and downward ╲ inflections. Examples.

ANTAGONISM OF GRAMMATICAL FORMS.

Analysis of Interrogation:

1. The "interrogative form" is antagonistic to the spirit when requiring to be read with the *downward* inflection, being *assertive* in meaning. Examples.

Sentences *in part* declarative, in part interrogative.

2. The "conditional form" is opposed to the "spirit," and requires to be read with the downward ╲, when the thought is *absolute*.

3. The "imperative form" is opposed to the "spirit," when requiring to be read with the *upward* inflection, the thought being conditional, uncertain. Examples.

MELODY.

As applied to the reading of poetry. Faults against melody.

Common defects to be avoided:
    1. Similarity of "rhythmical accent."
    2.   "   " "ending."
    3.   " by pause.

These are subdivided. Examples.

Tones of the Emotions.

The symbol of sublimity, the grand, the majestic, etc., the "Orotund." Examples.

The symbol of love, tenderness, affection, the Diminuendo, >—. Imperceptible vanish. Illustrations.

Symbol of sorrow, grief, penitence, etc., the Semitone. Examples.

Symbol of anger, wrath, etc., abrupt force. Exercise for giving strength, volume, dignity to the voice. Exercise on abrupt force, the skillful execution of which (abrupt force) is one of the highest vocal attainments, and becomes a security against injury to the throat in speaking.

Symbols of aversion, praise, joy, sarcasm, etc. The Aspirate symbol of earnestness, hate, etc. Exercises for each

Gesture.

Natural principles for each gesture. Grace—how expressed. Energy—where and when employed. Affirmative, negative, rejection, propulsion, pointing, elevation or depression, deferention, description, extended, literal gestures. Appropriate passages on which to exercise each.

CONTENTS.

CHAPTER I.
PAGE
CULTIVATION OF THE VOICE.—1st Scale, 2d Scale, 3d Scale, 4th Scale, 5th Scale..... 15

CHAPTER II.
TIME.—Parenthesis, Simile, Quotation, Metaphor, Marvellous. 28

CHAPTER III.
EMPHASIS.—Parables, Massing, Transfer, Mental Projection, Antagonism of Grammatical Forms...................... 65

CHAPTER IV.
INFLECTION.—Psychological Positives and Negatives, The Wave of the Voice..................................... 88

CHAPTER V.
THE TONES OF THE EMOTIONS.—Sorrow, Symbol of Joy, Surprise, Sublimity, etc., etc.......................... 125

CHAPTER VI.
GESTURE.—Grace, Energy, etc., etc........ 168

CHAPTER VII.
MISCELLANEOUS EXAMPLES............................... 204

CHAPTER I.

CULTIVATION OF THE VOICE.

THE speaking or reading voice is capable of improvement in the same proportion as the singing voice; and we can all appreciate the degree of excellence attained by our "prime donne," our tenors and bassos. We may also compare the same voice in its uncultivated state with the pitch of perfection to which culture has brought it, and involuntarily exclaim with the poet: "This was beautiful, but *this* is Beauty; this was strong, but *this* is Strength; this was perfect, this is Perfection."

To express the various emotions, the contrasts frequently portrayed in a poem, to read a character from a play, or to personate in one reading or recitation several characters, requires a command of tones, a pliancy of voice, seldom in the power of those who have daily practice only on the limited range of notes, called into play by the every day interchange of thought, the question and the answer of ordinary life; and these can be attained only by the most careful and comprehensive vocal culture, in accordance with principles which we shall try to make plain in the progress of this book.

To cultivate the voice we must acquire—

1. Flexibility, which consists of a smooth and easy gliding from one note to another.

2. A good "range" or "compass," so that the voice may with ease run up to a very high note, or take, without effort or straining, a very deep, round, resonant tone.

3. An improved *quality* of voice, which can only be obtained through culture.

In the exercises which follow, all the practice that is necessary for the acquirement of these objects can be obtained; but they must be faithfully studied and practised—no merely theoretical knowledge is of the slightest service here. The various illustrative passages are selected on the following principles, which must be borne in mind in order to understand this and the immediately succeeding lessons:

1. When practice is desired on a "scale" in which the voice may slide though a whole tone to the next in order, lines are chosen in which the quantity is capable of indefinite prolongation—a vowel, or vowels, being contained in each syllable.

2. To compel the voice to rise by "steps" instead of the gliding movement, lines are selected for the predominance of their sounding consonants.

3. For practice on the "semitonic" movement, lines in which the sentiments of regret, pity, or grief are predominant, will be best adapted for giving us power and ease in the expression of those emotions.

FIRST SCALE.

The first scale is for practice on whole notes; the "range" neither so high nor so low that beginners will find difficulty in taking it.

Claudio. Is this the monument of Leonato?
Attendant. It is, my lord.
Claud. (*Reads from a scroll.*)
    Done to death by slanderous tongues,
      Was the Hero that here lies:
    Death, in guerdon of her wrongs
      Gives her fame, which never dies;
So the life that died with shame,
Lives in death with glorious fame,
Hang thou there upon the tomb,
              (affixing it)
Praising her when I am dumb.
          —*Much Ado about Nothing.*

Commencing where Claudio reads from a scroll, "Done to death," recite those three words on a high brilliant key on one tone. Then throwing the voice quite five tones lower, pronounce the same words again, in fuller, rounder tones; then, throwing the voice *as low as possible*, beginning with the word "Done," rise gradually until the word "dies" has been pronounced; give the word "So" on the same "tone," then gradually descend.

As in the harp the vibrations are more numerous on the shorter strings, fewer and longer on the longer strings, in the "speaking voice" there is greater acuteness and more vibrations on the higher tones, and greater gravity and fewer vibrations on the lower tones.

The following arrangement will assist the pupil in the practice of this scale:

```
                    dies    4 So the
                    never     life
                    which     that
                    fame      died
                    her       with
1 Done to death!    gives     shame
                    wrongs    lives
                    of her    in death
                    in guerdon with
                    Death     glorious
          lies                fame
          here                hang
          that                thou
          Hero   2 Done to death there
          the                 upon
          was                 the tomb
          tongues             praising
          sland'rous          her
        by                    when
      death                   I
    to                        am
3 Done                        dumb.
```

Bear in mind that the voice is not to be unnaturally strained. After sufficient practice the voice may be able to rise or fall only the fourth of a tone above or below what was formerly its power; yet that is something gained, and *must* be acquired by long practice, never by forcing.

There are some defects in the practice of scales, into

which the beginner may be betrayed, if he be not cautious, and which, on being warned, the keen, critical or sensitive ear will carefully avoid.

1. In ascending the scale do not "economize" by rising a few tones, then falling or going back a little; then ascending again a short distance, only to retrograde once more after a few seconds; this false mode of practising we may exemplify in the following manner:

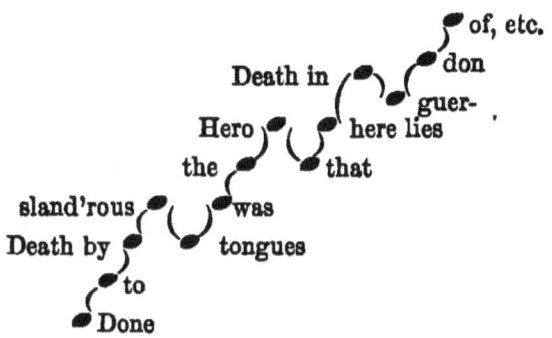

This fault is usually committed by people with a conscious inability to rise to a very high pitch.

2. Listen attentively to your own voice in ascending, and make sure that you are doing so gradually and regularly. Do not, through inadvertence, allow the voice to skip a note or two; this mistake is made by people of defective "ear"—those of whom we speak as not having a "good ear" for music. The same care should be observed in descending the scale, as an involuntary "skip" may be made through inattention. When this fault is committed, the pupil will find that, before a sentence of his scale has been pronounced, he has reached the highest tone of which his voice is capable, and *vice versa* in the descent.

CULTIVATION OF THE VOICE.

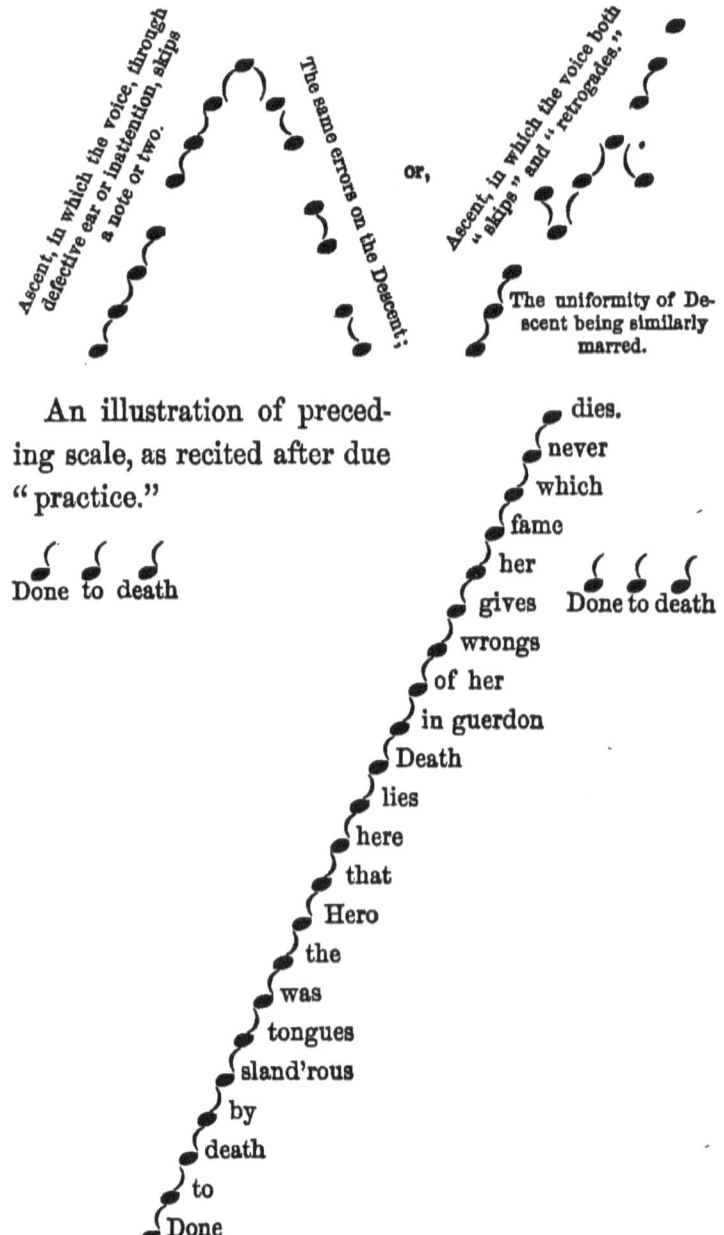

An illustration of preceding scale, as recited after due "practice."

CULTIVATION OF THE VOICE.

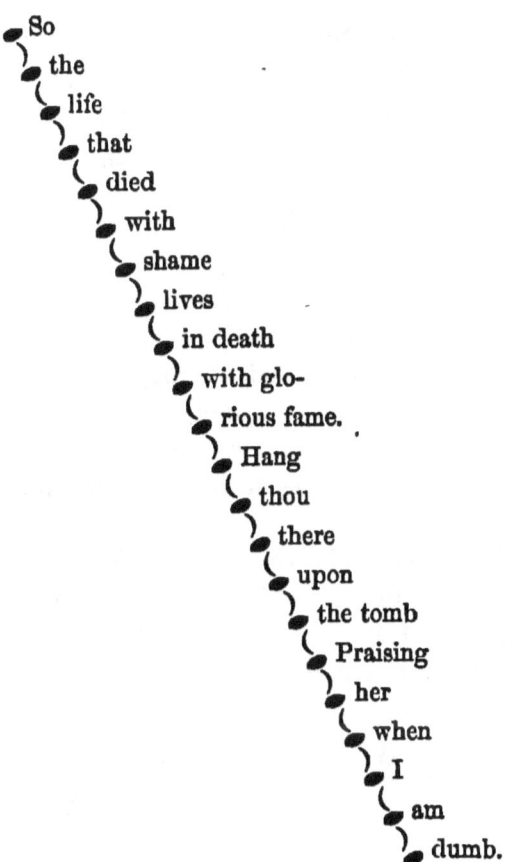

In this scale, dwell on the vowel sounds; you will then carry the voice almost without breakage by the gliding movement from tone to tone throughout.

SECOND SCALE.

The same directions for practice are to be followed here as in previous scale; for certain voices this may be found an easier scale for practice at first than the preceding. A voice that with difficulty takes the upper notes, had better begin with the second scale; but after a certain facility has been attained with the first, those having a deficiency in deep notes had better give especial attention to this one.

Puck. How now, spirit : whither wander you ?
Fairy. Over hill, over dale,
    Thorough bush, thorough brier,
  Over park, over pale,
    Thorough flood, thorough fire,
I do wander every where,
Swifter than the moones sphere.
                 —*Midsummer Night's Dream.*

Recite the first line on a high brilliant tone; allowing the voice to fall a tone on the last syllable of "wander," and again a "tone" on "you," in order to form a pleasing cadence.

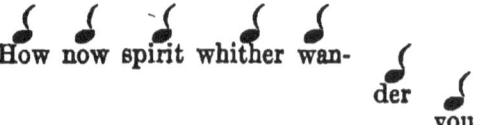

Commencing "Over hill" on the ordinary conversational key, rise gradually until you have pronounced the word "fire;" give "I" on the same tone as "fire," then descend, each succeeding tone being deeper, fuller, and longer than the last, until at the word "sphere," the lowest tone in the compass of the voice is reached.

The same precautions as to the avoidance of certain faults in practice apply to this as to the first scale.

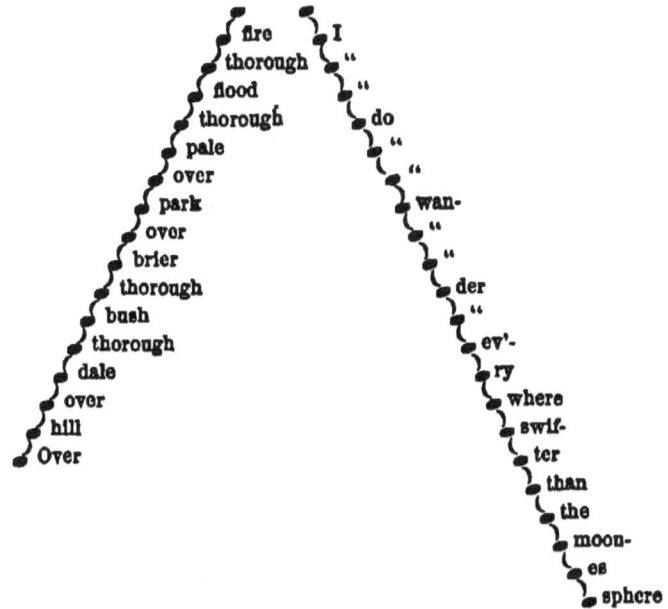

On the descent the voice should have attained a point in its compass quite five tones lower than the note on which "over" was given.

THIRD SCALE.

I now introduce a passage to be employed, first as a scale, then as an exercise for obtaining distinctness of utterance. As a scale, the voice rises, not by the gliding movement, but by "steps," giving all the consonants great prominence. As an exercise on "Distinctness," read the lines in a natural manner, but dwell on each vowel, and give all the consonants great force and prominence, especially "C" having the sound of "K," "R," "T," "P," "D."

24 CULTIVATION OF THE VOICE.

"The raging rocks,
With shivering shocks,
Shall break the locks,
 Of prison-gates:
And Phibbus' car
Shall shine from far,
And make and mar
 The foolish fates."
—*Midsummer Night's Dream.*

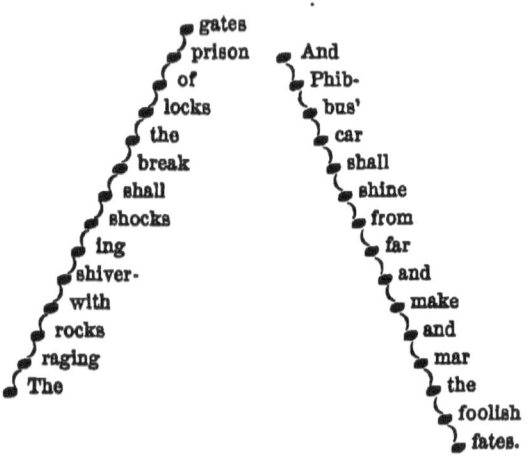

FOURTH SCALE.

The arrangement is similar to Scale 2. The range of voice, however, is both higher and lower than in that scale. The voice should have had ample practice on the preceding exercises before this one is attempted.

Titania. Come, now a roundel, and a fairy song;
Then, for the third part of a minute, hence;
Some to kill cankers in the musk-rose buds;
Some, war with rear-mice for their leathern wings,

CULTIVATION OF THE VOICE. 25

To make my small elves coats ; and some, keep back
The clamorous owl, that nightly hoots, and wonders
At our quaint spirits : Sing me now asleep ;
Then to your offices, and let me rest.
                    —*Midsummer Night's Dream.*

Practice this scale many times before attempting any force; giving the whole attention to acquiring a "true" ascent and descent.

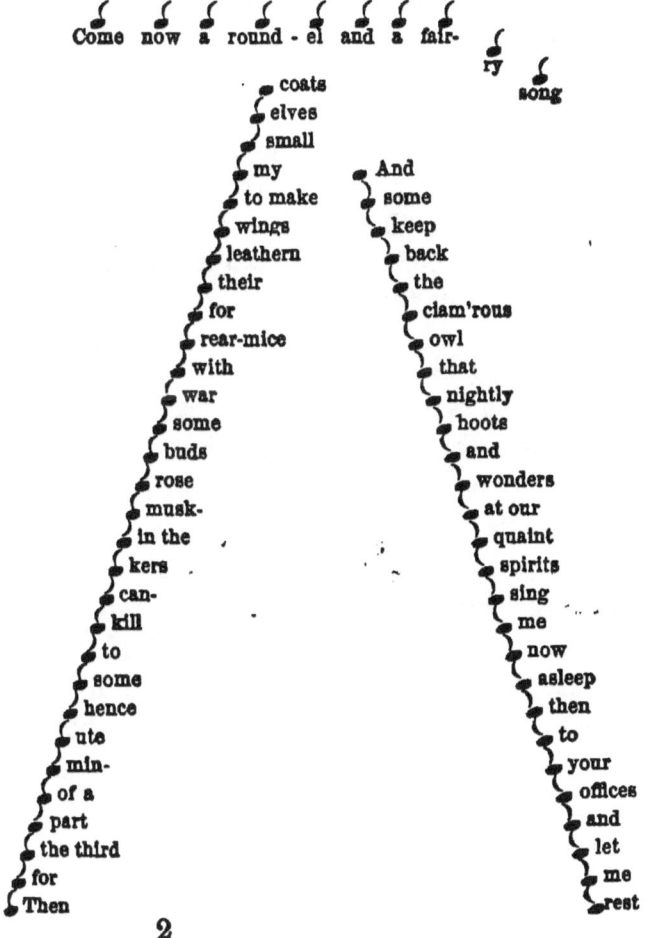

Exercise for Practice of Distinct Utterance.

The following passage embraces the quality of intensity of expression which requires a certain degree of the "Aspirate."

Calaban. As wicked dew as e'er my mother brush'd
With raven's feather from unwholesome fen,
Drop on you both! a south-west blow on ye,
And blister you all o'er!
Prospero. For this, be sure, to-night thou shalt have
    cramps,
Side-stitches that shall pen thy breath up; urchins
Shall, for that vast of night that they may work,
All exercise on thee: thou shalt be pinch'd
As thick as honey-combs, each pinch more stinging
Than bees that made them.
—*The Tempest.*

Give Calaban a deep, guttural voice, sounding each consonant very forcibly. When Prospero speaks, his words call for the aspirate combined with great stress on the consonant, to give his speech the degree of earnestness and energy its sentiments call for.

In their proper place the "Symbols" of the different "Emotions" will be given and described. In passages appropriated simply for "Cultivation of Voice," but little mention will be made of these symbols.

CULTIVATION OF THE VOICE. 27

FIFTH SCALE.

1 To the deep!

    3 Down

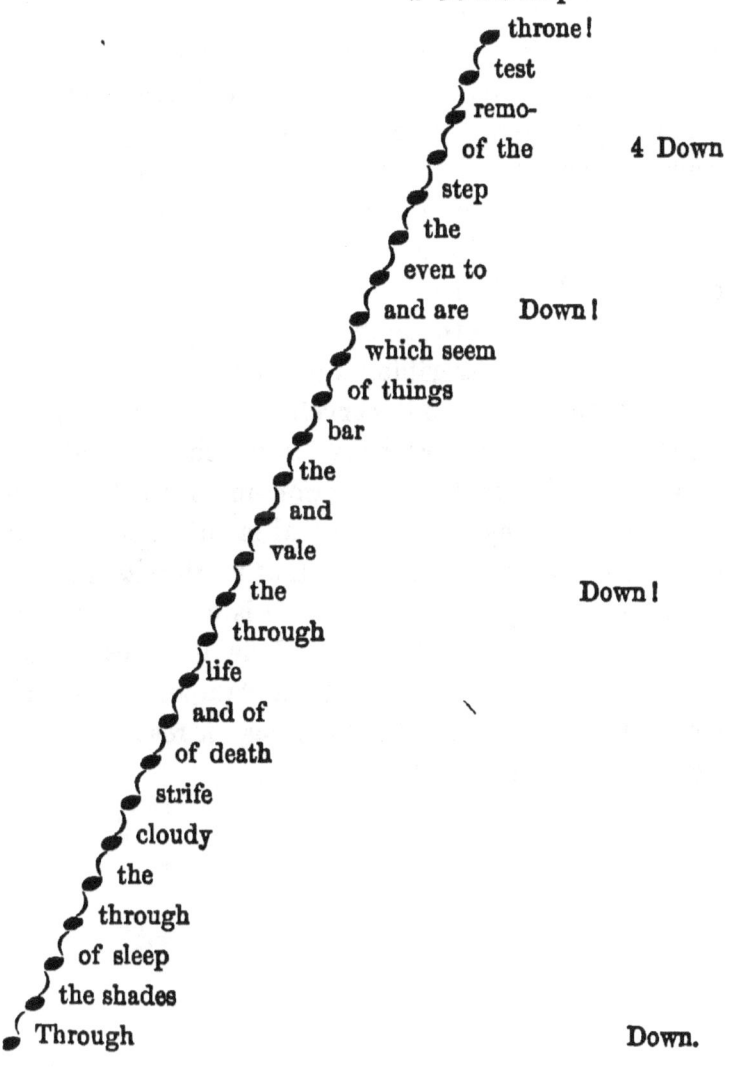

                      2 To the deep
                        throne!
                        test
                    remo-
                of the   4 Down
                step
              the
            even to
          and are   Down!
        which seem
       of things
      bar
      the
     and
    vale
   the
  through   Down!
 life
and of
of death
strife
cloudy
the
through
of sleep
the shades
Through   Down.

CHAPTER II.

TIME.

ONE of the most important means for interpreting an author correctly is varied "*time*" in utterance. The longer or shorter duration of time occupied in the rendering of sentences, expresses the *mental valuation* of such sentences; and the *relative changes* in "time," the relative importance of the various passages. The relationship of groups of clauses, also, is indicated "by time." The train of literal thought which is interrupted by a metaphor, is depicted as such by a difference in the "time" between literal and metaphorical, symbolizing the natural "break" in the thought.

That you are describing a miracle, the accomplishment of prophecy, the marvellous, etc., etc., is indicated by the particular "time" in which you read. A parable is a figurative illustration in which the direct or literal meaning is not the real or principal one; it is designed to point an important truth with greater vividness; then, as the illustration is not so important as that which it illustrates as a whole, it is read faster than that which it images, and the "important truth" which it points—that is, the teaching—is read in slower time than the main text.

Students in elocution are frequently told (and they gather the same impression from books on the subject) "that the parenthesis is read in faster time than the rest of the sentence."—That this is a gross mistake as to certain kinds of parentheses, I will proceed to show.

Paul, an apostle, (not of men, neither by man, but by Jesus Christ, and God the Father, who raised him from the dead ;)
And all the brethren which are with me, unto the churches of Galatia.—*Gal.* 1 : 6.

Is the fact that Paul and the brethren with him speak unto the churches of Galatia, of more importance, than the fact that Paul is "not of men, neither by man, but by Jesus Christ, and God the Father, who raised him from the dead ?" "Certainly not," you say, "it is of less importance than the parenthesis." In that case, do you convey your mental valuation of the important parenthesis by reading it in *faster* time than the main text? You do not; but by reading it in much "slower" time than the lines immediately preceding and succeeding it, you at once indicate the mental value with which you regard it, or in other words, its superiority in importance to the main text. Another example :

7 But contrariwise, when they saw that the gospel of the uncircumcision was committed unto me, as the gospel of the circumcision was unto Peter ;

8 (For he that wrought effectually in Peter to the apostleship of the circumcision, the same was mighty in me toward the Gentiles :)

9 And when James, Cephas, and John, who seemed to be pillars, perceived the grace that was given unto me, they gave to me and Barnabas the right hands of fellowship; that we should go unto the heathen, and they unto the circumcision.—*Gal.* 2 : 5, 7–9.

That the same mighty God was as effectual in Paul, as in Peter, being manifestly of greater importance than the main text, the 8th v. will be properly "valued" by a rendering in "slower time."

And here is a still more forcible example:—

4 But God, who is rich in mercy, for his great love wherewith he loved us,

5 Even when we were dead in sins, hath quickened us together with Christ, (by grace ye are saved;)

6 And hath raised us up together, and made us sit together in heavenly places in Christ Jesus :—*Ephes.*, ch. 2.

The beautiful parenthesis, "By grace ye are saved," has its full meaning and value given, when read twice as slowly as the main text. The practice that many have, of reading the parenthesis in faster time, would in this case argue an absolute making light, or little, of the "saving grace."

The rule, then, as regards the duration of "time" in rendering the parenthesis is: "*The parenthesis is read in slower time, when superior, and faster, when inferior, in importance to the main text.*

In the subjoined example we have two parentheses; the first, "Whereto the rather shall his day's hard journey soundly invite him," being inferior, requires the faster time.

The second, "When we have marked with blood those sleepy two of his own chamber, and used their very daggers" is superior to the rest of the passage, and consequently is read in slower time.

Macbeth. If we should-fail,——
Lady Macb. We fail!
But screw your courage to the sticking-place,
And we'll not fail. When Duncan is asleep,
(Whereto the rather shall his day's hard journey
Soundly invite him,) his two chamberlains
Will I with wine and wassel so convince,
That memory, the warder of the brain,
Shall be a fume, and the receipt of reason
A limbeck only. When in swinish sleep
Their drenched natures lie, as in a death,
What cannot you and I perform upon
The unguarded Duncan? what not put upon
His spongy officers, who shall bear the guilt
Of our great quell?
Macb. Bring forth men-children only!
For thy undaunted metal should compose
Nothing but males. Will it not be received,
(When we have mark'd with blood those sleepy two
Of his own chamber, and used their very daggers,)
That they have done't?

Towards the end of Hamlet's long speech at the conclusion of Act 2, Sc. 2, occurs the lines—

"The spirit that I have seen
May be a devil; (and the devil hath power
To assume a pleasing shape): yea, and perhaps

Out of my weakness, and my melancholy,
(As he is very potent with such spirits)
Abuses me to damn me."

Both parentheses are inferior to the main text, being merely reflections and repetitions of a fact or facts that are patent to all—the devil having power to assume a pleasing shape being no new fact to us nor to Hamlet; and that "he is very potent" conveys no new idea. In each case, if read twice as fast as the lines preceding and succeeding them, the relative value of these inferior parentheses compared with the more important main text is shown at once.

In this passage from one of the "Ingoldsby Legends," the meaning would be extremely obscure were it not for the necessary changes in "time":

" [4]You may fancy King Charles at some court fancy ball
[2](The date we may fix in sixteen sixty-six,
In the room built by Inigo Jones at Whitehall,
Whence his father the martyr [8](as such mourned by all
Who in his wept the laws' and the monarchy's fall)
[3]Stepped out to exchange regal robes for a pall)—
[4]You may fancy King Charles, I say, stopping the brawl
As burst on his sight the old church of St. Paul,
By the light of its flames now beginning to crawl
From basement to buttress and topping its wall."

The peculiarity here is a parenthesis within a parenthesis; the whole of the longer one, with the exception of the one contained, being inferior, while the interpolation is superior to the preceding and succeeding lines. To mark the relative value of main text and the inferior and superior parentheses, I have placed the figures "4," "2," "8" in their respective places. No. 4 indicates the ordinary time in which the passage is begun; No. 2, at the beginning of the inferior parenthesis, where the time should be twice as fast; No. 8, at the commencement of the slow parenthesis, which indicates that it should be given twice as slowly as the lines read in "ordinary" or "4" time.

As to the *manner* of reading in "slow" or in "fast" time, there is an "unnatural" and a "natural" method; the first-named, which we wish, of course, to avoid, is commonly that of making pauses between words, for the purpose of attaining to a "slowness" in the rendering. This is a mistake; it is not what we do naturally when we speak slowly. The "natural" method of speaking slowly is by *dwelling on the vowel sounds* in words for a longer or shorter interval as may be necessary.

§ 1.—THE SIMILE.

In what kind of "time" should the "simile" be read? We employ "similes," in writing or speaking, for giving to the mind's eye a picture, a resemblance, of the thought or object described. We indicate the attitude of mind toward that described, by the *sort* of comparison we make. In a word, we express either "approbation" or disapprobation of the thoughts or objects spoken of, when making use of that which we term a "likeness" of the thought or object. In reading, as we give that "comparison" in slower or in faster time than the main text, do we express either approbation or disapprobation. Not only so, but a simile should be isolated by a pause before the word introducing the comparison, and another pause at the conclusion; for the simile is a picture of the thought, and a picture should be entire—presented on one piece of canvas—not the girl dipping her pitcher represented on one side of the room, and the well from which she draws her water, on another. Word-painting, like color-painting, must present a thought complete.

Sometimes a number of similes follow one another, to each of which the thought or object is compared; but each one is a picture in itself, and should be presented as such by isolating it from the main text; yet, by a delicate attention to time, the various similes can be presented, as a series of pictures referring to a special thought are in an art-gallery; they should be read carefully, and in quick and close proximity, yet kept distinct from each other.

The æsthetic principle of time, as applied to elocution, is this: *naturally*, in giving expression to thoughts of approbation, of importance, of superiority, etc., etc., taste directs us to speak in slower time; we all do this, most of us not noticing that we do so. The same rule of taste which compels the slower time in these cases, requires *faster* time when describing thoughts the opposite of these—disapprobation, unimportance, inferiority, etc.

Some persons make it a rule to read the "simile" in slower time indiscriminately. This is an error, as an illustration will show: "Though I speak with the tongues of men and of angels, and have not charity, I am become—as sounding brass or a tinkling cymbal." —1 *Cor.* 13 : 1. Observe, that by reading this simile in slower time than the main text, the ear is misled into dwelling upon the importance of the "sounding brass and tinkling cymbal;" you would indicate, as it were, approbation, instead of the disapprobation, which is plainly the writer's intention. By isolating the simile, by reading it as a unit throughout, and in time twice as fast as the remainder of the passage, you convey the author's disapprobation of those who are as "sounding brass," etc., through lack of charity.

Superficial readers, having made themselves familiar with this principle of time, must not be betrayed into reading in slower time certain similes, simply because of those similes being beautiful in themselves, when they are compared to the subject merely to show disapprobation, as in Hosea 13 : 3 :

"Therefore they shall be [as the morning cloud] and [as the early dew that passeth away]."

After Israel's sins he is to be *punished* by passing away as quickly as the morning cloud or the early dew; but careless readers are apt to glance only at the beauty of the "morning cloud," the sweetness of the "early dew," not regarding the reason for making the comparison, which is that Israel's course shall be as short, as fleeting as they. The disapprobation is immediately indicated by the faster time in which both similes should be read. The remainder of the comparisons in the same verse—

"As the chaff that is driven with the whirlwind out of the floor, and [as the smoke out of the chimney]"—

are, it is at once perceived, disapprobatory.

Hosea 14 : 5, 6, 7, furnish similes of approbation, and immediately does the beautiful rendering of them in "slow" time portray the *mercy* that God is now disposed to show to Israel:

"I will be [as the dew] unto Israel, he shall grow [as the lily] and cast forth his roots [as Lebanon]. His branches shall spread, and his beauty shall be [as the olive tree,]" etc., etc.

In Psalm 1 : 3 :

"And he shall be [like a tree planted by the rivers of water, that bringeth forth his fruit in his season]; his leaf also shall [not wither] ; and whatsoever he doeth shall prosper."

That he who practices "goodness" shall be rewarded is intimated by the slow time of the simile, before the hearer's understanding grasps the meaning of the words. In verse 4 an opposite result is attained by the rapidity of rendering:

"[1]The ungodly are not so, but are [²like the chaff which the wind driveth away]

In Proverbs 1 : 9 the usual introductory "as" or "like," before the simile, is understood; so that the distinct pause comes directly before the simile itself:

"For they shall be [an ornament of grace unto thy head] and [chains about thy neck]."

The comparative littleness of all earthly things in the eyes of God is in the same manner expressed by the change to fast time:

"Behold the nations are [as a drop of a bucket]; and are counted [as the small dust of the balance]; behold he taketh up the isles [as a very little thing]."—*Isaiah* 40:15.

A simile which is used in describing that which we admire, is naturally given in slower time than the remainder of the text; those also that picture the grand, the sublime, the majestic, the solemn, the beautiful, the holy, love (in the better sense), etc. In each case this *slowness* intimates approbation. Similes portraying their opposites, dislike, the despicable, the tawdry, the ridiculous, the mean, the superficial, the hideous, the ugly, the unholy, sensuality, etc., require the faster time, which indicates disapprobation even before the peculiar meaning of the words has penetrated to the brain of the hearer at all. In each case the writer's (or supposed speaker's) *purpose* is understood to be depicted, pointing out *his* approbation or disapprobation, not *yours*.

It is evident from the preceding exposition that these changes in time cannot be too highly valued. In listening to the reading of others, we have no leisure for examining the author's special meaning; the memory may retrace its steps but for a fleeting instant. Poetry gives us constant inversions of phrases and sentences, and for depicting the relationship of words or sentences thus treated, a uniformly slow or fast time would be entirely inadequate. Judicious pauses on the part of the reader, and again the careful connection of lines or sentences, are required to give the author's meaning.

Wolsey, the "bright and shining light," finds that he is to be extinguished as suddenly as is the "bright exhalation in the evening;" his deprecation of such ending, and the ignominy attendant, are fitly described by the rapid "time" in which the simile is spoken.

> Nay, then, farewell!
> I have touch'd the highest point of all my greatness;
> And, from that full meridian of my glory,
> I haste now to my setting : I shall fall
> [Like a bright exhalation in the evening],
> And no man see me more.—*Henry VIII.*

"As rolls a thousand waves to a rock, so Swaran's host came on; as meets a rock a thousand waves, so Inisfail met Swaran."—*Fingal, Book I.*

The second simile is of approbation—plainly the slow time will show that unimpregnable nature of the stand of Inisfail; and the faster time on the first comparison portrays the impotent fury of Swaran's host.

The music was [like the memory of joys that are past] pleasant and mournful to the soul.—*Ossian.*

The simile is given with approbation.

Queen. What, is my Richard both in shape and mind Transform'd, and weaken'd? Hath Bolingbroke

Deposed thine intellect? Hath he been in thy heart?
[The lion, dying, thrusteth forth his paw,
And wounds the earth, if nothing else, with rage
To be o'erpower'd;] and wilt thou, pupil-like,
Take thy correction mildly? kiss the rod;
And fawn on rage with base humility
Which art a *lion*, and a king of beasts?
—*Richard II.*

The queen's approbation of the lion's daring effort at revenge, though impotent, is indicated by the slowness of time in which we give the sentence as far as "o'erpowered;" then, her disapprobation of Richard's "kissing the rod" is shown by rapidity. A principle of intonation is particularly exemplified here. It is explained under the section, "Inflections of Voice."

"Sorrow [like a cloud on the sun] shades the soul of Dessamoor."—*Ossian.*

If the image describes that which is disagreeable or irksome, as it does in this instance, faster time is required in rendering it.

In the following the simile is not beautiful, but it describes exactly the bitter medicine which carries health with it, and consequently something that is *good* for us:

"Sweet are the *uses* of adversity, which,
 [Like the toad ugly and venomous,
 Wears yet a precious jewel in his head]."

In Richard II, Act 1, Scene 4, the similes are of

approbation, though at a casual glance one might suppose the contrary:

Gard. They are; and Bolingbroke
Hath seized the wasteful king.—Oh! what pity is it,
That he had not so trimm'd and dress'd his land,
[As we this garden? We at time of year
Do wound the bark, the skin of our fruit-trees;
Lest, being over-proud with sap and blood,
With too much riches it confound itself] :
Had he done so to great and growing men,
They might have lived to bear, and he to taste
Their fruits of duty. [All superfluous branches
We lop away, that bearing boughs may live :]
Had he done so, himself had borne the crown,
Which waste of idle hours hath quite thrown down.

A simile of approbation. In this (as in the preceding example) is illustrated the principle of "Inflection" I have mentioned.

As the bright stars and milky way,
Showed by the night, are hid by day,
So we in that accomplished mind
(Helped by the night) *new* graces find,
Which by the splendor of her view
Dazzled before, we never knew.
— *Waller.*

Vio. A blank, my lord. She never told her love,
But let concealment, [like a worm i' the bud],
Feed on her damask cheek: she pined in thought;
And, with a green and yellow melancholy,

She sat [like Patience on a monument],
Smiling at grief.   Was not this love, indeed?
We men may say more, swear more : but, indeed,
Our shows are more than will ; for still we prove
Much in our vows, but little in our love.
— *Twelfth Night.*

Both similes here require the faster time.

In the next example the simile begins at "Even," and ends at "tongue;" it should be read as a unit, and the spirit of the passage requires "fast" time.

North. How doth my son, and brother?
Thou tremblest ; and the whiteness in thy cheek
Is apter than thy tongue to tell thy errand.
Even such a man, so faint, so spiritless,
So dull, so dead in look, so wo-begone,
Drew Priam's curtain in the dead of night,
And would have told him, half his Troy was burn'd ;
But Priam found the fire, ere he his tongue,
And I my Percy's death, ere thou report'st it.
This thou wouldst say,—" Your son did thus, and thus;
Your *brother*, thus ; *so* fought the noble *Douglas;*"
Stopping my greedy ear with their bold deeds :
But in the end, to stop mine ear *indeed,*
Thou hast a *sigh* to blow away this praise,
Ending with—brother, son, and all are dead.
— *Part 2, Henry IV.*

In this, Iliad xx. 569, the "Hero" is greatly elevated by the comparison ; slow time is appropriate.

"[As when a flame the winding valley fills,
And runs on crackling shrubs between the hills,
Then o'er the stubble, up the mountain flies,
Fires the high woods and blazes to the skies,
This way and that the spreading torrent roars];
So sweeps the hero through the washed shores.
Around him, wide, immense destruction pours,
And earth is deluged with the sanguine showers."

In the lines that follow, the simile gives us an idea of the grandeur of Hector's valor. Slowness of time is then necessary for correct interpretation.

"Thus breathing death in terrible array,
The close compacted legions urged their way;
Fierce they drove on, impatient to destroy;
Troy charged the first, and *Hector* first of Troy.
[As from some mountain's craggy forehead torn,
A rock's round fragment flies; with fury borne
(Which from the stubborn stone a torrent rends)
Precipitate the pond'rous mass descends;
From steep to steep the rolling ruin bounds,
At every shock the crackling wood resounds!
Still gathering force, it smokes; and urged amain,
Whirls, leaps, and thunders down impetuous to the plain;
There stops]—so Hector. Their whole force he proved;
Resistless when he raged; and when he stopt, unmoved."

The "ridiculous" is pointed out by the faster time in which this comparison is read:

"Hélas! l'amour m'a pris
  [Comme le chat fait la souris]."

In Longfellow's charming poem—Evangeline, are found numerous fine examples. I append a few:

The murmuring pines and the hemlocks
Bearded with moss, and with garments green, indistinct in the twilight
Stand [like druids of old, with voices sad and prophetic],
Stand [like harpers hoar with beards that rest on their bosoms],
Loud from its rocky caverns the deep-voiced neighboring ocean
Speaks, and in accents disconsolate answers the wail of the forest.
* * * * Men whose lives glided on—[like rivers that water the woodlands] * * * * Scattered,—[like dust and leaves], etc. * * * * When she had passed it seemed—[like the ceasing of exquisite music] * * * * Sweet was her breath—[as the breath of kine that feed in the meadows] * * * * Stalworth and stately in form was the man of seventy winters; Hearty and hale was he, [an oak that is covered with snowflakes]. * * * * Bent, [like a laboring oar that toils in the surf of the ocean], Bent, (but not broken) by age was the form of the notary public; * * * * Silently one by one, in the infinite meadows of heaven, Blossomed the lovely stars—[the forget-me-nots of the angels]. * * * * And as she gazed from the window, she saw serenely the moon pass forth from the folds of a cloud, and one star follow her footsteps—[as out of Abraham's tent young Ishmael wandered with Hagar]!

* * * * * * *

"Prisoners now I declare you; for such is his Majesty's pleasure!

[As when the air is serene in the sultry solstice of summer
Suddenly gathers a storm, and the deadly sling of the
 hailstones
Beats down the farmer's corn in the field and shatters his
 windows,
Hiding the sun and strewing the ground with thatch
 from the house-roofs;
Bellowing fly the herds, and seek to break their inclo-
 sures];
So on the hearts of the people descended the words of the
 speakers."

For practising the rendering of the simile I would specially recommend Shelley's "Skylark," Milton's "Paradise Lost," Book I, 331; Book IV, 178; Book III, 540; Book IV, 797, and many other passages from the same poem. Longfellow's "Evangeline" may be studied from the beginning to the end for this practice. Many of the psalms afford excellent illustrations. In some of Willis's sacred poems the reader may find charming examples of the "simile"; I will mention "Jairus' daughter," "The Leper," and "Absalom" as being among the best for the purpose.

§ 2.—THE QUOTATION.

When the quotation is superior in importance to the main text, we give it in slower "time"; if it is inferior to that going before, and coming after, we read it more rapidly. The quotation is, of course, always *faster* when intended for "disparagement," whether superior to the main text or not. Whether the quotation be directly illustrative, or only indirectly, it is marked by change in time (and a corresponding change of voice, or tone).

To illustrate, take the following from the second chapter of Matthew:

1 Now when Jesus was born in Bethlehem of Judea in the days of Herod the king, behold, there came wise men from the east to Jerusalem,

2 Saying, "Where is he that is born King of the Jews? for we have seen his star in the east, and are come to worship him."

3 When Herod the king had heard these things, he was troubled, and all Jerusalem with him.

4 And when he had gathered all the chief priests and scribes of the people together, he demanded of them "where Christ should be born."

5 And they said unto him, "In Bethlehem of Judea: for thus it is written by the prophet,"

6 "And thou Bethlehem, in the land of Juda, art not the least among the princes of Juda: for out of thee shall come a Governor, that shall rule my people Israel."

7 Then Herod, when he had privily called the wise men, enquired of them diligently "what time the star appeared."

8 And he sent them to Bethlehem, and said, "Go and. search diligently for the young child; and when ye have found him, bring me word again, that *I* may come and worship him also."

A "retarded time" is natural in describing the marvelous. See section on Wonder, etc.

9 When they had heard the king, they departed; and, lo, the star, which they saw in the east, went before them, till it came and stood over where the young child was.

10 When they saw the star, they rejoiced with exceeding great joy.

11 And when they were come into the house, they saw the young child with Mary his mother, and fell down, and worshipped him: and when they had opened their treasures, they presented unto him gifts; gold, and frankincense, and myrrh.

12 And being warned of God in a dream that they should *not* return to Herod, they departed into their own country another way.

13 And when they were departed, behold, the angel of the Lord appeareth to Joseph in a dream, saying, "Arise, and take the young child and his mother, and flee into Egypt, and be thou there until I bring thee word: for Herod will seek the young child to destroy him."

14 When he arose, he took the young child and his mother by night, and departed into Egypt:

15 And was there until the death of Herod: that it might be fulfilled which was spoken of the Lord by the prophet, saying, "Out of Egypt have I called my son."

16 Then Herod, when he saw that he was mocked of the wise men, was exceeding wroth, and sent forth, and slew all the children that were in Bethlehem, and in all the coasts thereof, from two years old and under, according to the time which he had diligently enquired of the wise men.

17 Then was fulfilled that which was spoken by Jeremy the prophet, saying,

18 "In Rama was there a voice heard, lamentation,

and weeping, and great mourning, Rachel weeping for her children, and would not be comforted, because they are not.

19 But when Herod was dead, behold, an angel of the Lord appeareth in a dream to Joseph in Egypt,

20 Saying, " Arise, and take the young child and his mother, and go into the land of Israel: for they are dead which sought the young child's life."

21 And he arose, and took the young child and his mother, and came into the land of Israel.

22 But when he heard that Archelaus did reign in Judea in the room of his father Herod, he was afraid to go thither: (notwithstanding, being warned of God in a dream,) he turned aside into the parts of Galilee.

23 And he came and dwelt in a city called Nazareth: that it might be fulfilled which was spoken by the prophets, " He shall be called a Nazarene."

The quotation in this chapter (both direct and indirect) I have marked with inverted commas; they are all superior quotations, with the exception of those from Herod, whose motives in asking certain questions and in giving certain commands it is natural to disparage; these latter are rendered in faster time.

Many persons do not distinguish at all between the ordinary time of the main text and that of the quotation. I have heard people read these verses who seemed to regard the fact of John's unfashionable preference for a "garment of camel's hair and a leathern girdle," of equal importance with that which he preached: " Repent ye, for the kingdom of heaven is at hand; for this is he that was spoken of by the prophet Esaias, saying, 'The voice of one crying in the wilderness, Prepare ye the way of the Lord, make his paths straight.'" That John should be contented with plain "locusts" and "wild honey" they would appear to regard with as much astonishment (as far as any change in time is concerned), as the miraculous opening of the heavens and the "Spirit of God" descending like a dove upon Jesus, when John baptized him.

See the reading of the "marvellous" chapter.

In James 1 : 13 occurs the supposed quotation "I am tempted of God," which James certainly intends to disparage; his intention is effectually indicated by a change to fast time when reading it. Pupils will please remember, that the change in "time" must be distinguished by a change of "voice":

13 Let no man say when he is tempted, "I am tempted of God": for God cannot be tempted with evil, neither tempteth he any man.

In the third verse of the second chapter of James there are two quotations; the first is *superior*--there can be no objection to courtesy shown to the rich nor to any one; James disparages the contempt shown to the *poor*, by those who say to them, "Stand thou there, or sit here under my footstool":

3 And ye have respect to him that weareth the gay clothing, and say unto him, "Sit thou here in a good place;" and say to the poor, "Stand thou there, or sit here under my footstool."

We find a superior quotation in Rev. 22 : 6, 7;

reading also the first line of the eighth to show the change to ordinary time.

6 And he said unto me, "These sayings are faithful and true : and the Lord God of the holy prophets sent his angel to shew unto his servants the things which must shortly be done.
7 "Behold, I come quickly : blessed is he that keepeth the sayings of the prophecy of this book."
8 And I John saw these things, and heard them.

In Matt., ch. 4, there are examples of "fast" and "slow" quotations; the pupil should be required to read these verses, marking very carefully the change of time on each quotation, and the subsequent return to the main text; not forgetting that a change in time necessitates a change of tone :

1 Then was Jesus led up of the spirit into the wilderness to be tempted of the devil.
2 And when he had fasted forty days and forty nights, he was afterward an hungered.

Disparagement. Fast Time.

3 And when the tempter came to him, he said, "If thou be the Son of God, command that these stones be made bread."

Superior Quo. Slow Time.

4 But he answered and said, "It is written, Man shall not live by bread alone, but by every word that proceedeth out of the mouth of God."
5 Then the devil taketh him up into the holy city, and setteth him on a pinnacle of the temple.

Disparagement. Fast Time.

6 And saith unto him, "If thou be the Son of God, cast thyself down: for it is written, He shall give his angels charge concerning thee: and in their hands they shall bear thee up, lest at any time thou dash thy foot against a stone."

Superior Quo. Slow Time.

7 Jesus said unto him, "It is is written again, Thou shalt not tempt the Lord thy God."

8 Again, the devil taketh him up into an exceeding high mountain, and sheweth him all the kingdoms of the world, and the glory of them ;

Disparagement. Fast Time.

9 And saith unto him, "All these things will I give thee, if thou wilt fall down and worship me."

Superior Quo. Slow Time.

10 Then saith Jesus unto him, "Get thee hence, Satan : for it is written, Thou shalt worship the Lord thy God, and him only shalt thou serve."

11 Then the devil leaveth him, and, behold, angels came and ministered unto him.

Matt. 7 : 4, a quotation of disparagement:

4 Or how wilt thou say to thy brother, "Let me pull the mote out of thine eye "; and, behold, a beam is in thine own eye?

A quotation of disparagement. Ex., Matt., ch. 6.

31 Therefore take no thought, saying, " What shall we

eat? or, What shall we drink? or, Wherewithal shall we be clothed?"

32 (For after all these things do the Gentiles seek:) for your heavenly Father knoweth that ye have need of all these things.

Matt. 7 : 22, 23, displays examples of each, the first of disparagement, the second of superiority:

22 Many will say to me in that day, "Lord, Lord, have we not prophesied in thy name? and in thy name have cast out devils? and in thy name done many wonderful works?"

23 And then will I profess unto them, "I never knew you ; depart from me, ye that work iniquity."

In Matt., ch. 8, we have the beautiful story of the Centurion. How truly do we mark the simple faith in Jesus' almighty power by the slow rendering of the quotation in the sixth verse! and again, the Centurion's admirable humility (that virtue so dear to Jesus), by reading in slow time the quotation of the eighth verse. Then is the Lord's approbation of such faith and humility properly depicted to the mind's eye, by the slow time given to the quotations from the tenth and thirteenth verses:

5 And when Jesus was entered into Caper'naum, there came unto him a centurion, beseeching him,

6 And saying, Lord, my servant lieth at home sick of the palsy, grievously tormented.

7 And Jesus saith unto him, "I will come and heal him."

8 The centurion answered and said, "Lord, I am not worthy that thou shouldest come under my roof : but speak the word only, and my servant shall be healed."

* * * * * * * * *

10 When Jesus heard it, he marvelled, and said to them that followed, "Verily I say unto you, I have not found so great faith, no, not in Israel."

* * * * * * * * *

13 And Jesus said unto the centurion, "Go thy way ; and as thou hast believed so be it done unto thee." And his servant was healed in the selfsame hour.

It is necessary in each case to mark the *change* in "time" by reading a few words or lines *preceding* the quotation, and also a few words or lines coming after it. For *practising* the "time" of quotations, parenthesis, similes, etc., this observance is indispensable.

In the annexed examples, Matt., ch. 12, the Evangelist quotes the Pharisees disparagingly:

10 And, behold, there was a man which had his hand withered. And they asked him, saying, "Is it lawful to heal on the sabbath days?" that they might accuse him.

11 And he said unto them, "What man shall there be among you, that shall have one sheep, and if it fall into a pit on the sabbath day, will he not lay hold on it, and lift it out ?

12 "How much then is a man better than a sheep? Wherefore it is lawful to do well on the sabbath days."

13 Then saith he to the man, "Stretch forth thine hand." And he stretched it forth ; and it was restored whole, like as the other.

In the eleventh verse the "wave of the voice"—a natural principle explained under the heading, "Inflections of Voice"—is illustrated. Briefly, I will say, in passing, that these vacillating inflections answer to *mental* vacillations, the *mind* vacillating between the illustration and the object or subject it illustrates. In this case the illustration begins with the words, "What man shall there be among you," etc., ending with "lift it out"; the truth to which the illustration points being that "it is lawful to do good on the sabbath day." The direction of the "wave" may be thus illustrated : ⌣ ⌢ ⌣ ⌢ ⌣ ⌢. The "wave," you perceive, has not the force of the circumflex, ⌣ ⌢, nor the directness and energy of the upward and downward inflections, ╱ ╲.

§ 3.—THE METAPHOR.

A metaphor is the application of a word in some other than its ordinary use, on account of some resemblance between the functions of the two objects; thus, the President is said to be the "head" of the Republic because the head is the chief part of the body. The metaphor differs from the simile in form only; substantially they are the same. In the simile, the two subjects—that which is spoken of, and that to which it is compared—are quite distinct in *expression* as well as in thought; in the metaphor the two subjects are not distinct in form; the literal is carried directly into the metaphorical; yet, as there is necessarily a "break" in the thought between the literal and the metaphorical, and as we wish to read thoughts, not forms, or words only, there should be a corresponding "break" in the expression or rendering of the thought.

For instance, in the third chapter of Habakkuk, sixth verse:

"He stood—and measured the earth: he beheld—and drove asunder the nations: and the everlasting mountains—were scattered, the perpetual hills—did bow: his ways are everlasting."

"He stood" is or may be taken literally, but that literally he measured the earth with a "measure" would be absurd; "measured," then, is used in a metaphorical sense; the break in the "thought" is after the word stood, as the metaphor then begins.

He beheld—a break in thought—and drove asunder the nations; and the everlasting mountains—break in thought—were scattered; the perpetual hills—thought—did bow: "his ways are everlasting"—this last is, of course, all literal, and as such should be rendered.

"Then the moon shall be—confounded, and the sun—ashamed when the Lord of Hosts shall reign in Mount Zion, and in Jerusalem, and before his Ancients gloriously."—*Isaiah* 24 : 23.

After pronouncing the words, "Then the moon shall be," the mind reflects for an instant, in order to grasp a metaphorical image, which shall most keenly present the moon's change in appearance; no feeling presents a greater change in the human countenance than that of being utterly confounded, so that the mind instantly seizes upon a word which at once describes change of appearance in the animate object, and applies it to the inanimate. In the next line, in like manner, the predicted alteration in the sun's face is ascribed to "shame," an emotion which creates a marked difference of appearance in sentient beings, and so will most aptly describe the change in the sun.

In the following lines from the first part of Henry IV., Act 5, Sc. 9, Prince Henry assumes that glory and honor are a garland of flowers:

>   *Hotspur.*—Nor shall it, Harry, for the hour is come
> To end the one of us. And 'would to God,
> Thy name in arms were now as great as mine !
>   *Prince Henry.*—I'll make it greater, ere I part from
>   thee ;—
> —And all the budding honours on thy crest
> I'll crop, to make a garland for my head.

In the next from "Cymbeline," Act 3, Sc. 3, the break in the thought is after "I," in the sixth line. A man who had acquired great reputation and honors is supposed to be a tree loaded with fruit:

>   *Belarius.* O boys, this story the world,
> May read in me : my body's marked
> With Roman swords ; and my report was once
> First with the best of note : Cymbeline loved me ;
> And when a soldier was the theme, my name
> Was not far off : Then was I,—as a tree,

Whose boughs did bend with fruit : but in one night
A storm, or robbery, call it what you will,
Shook down my mellow hangings, nay, my leaves,
And left me bare to weather."

In Richard II., Act 1, Sc. 2, the first break in the thought is after the word "were"—when the mind seizes upon the metaphorical idea of Edward's being a tree, and his sons—seven fair branches, one of which has been cut down and his leaves all withered, etc., etc. The pause then comes after the word "were."

Duch. Finds brotherhood in thee no sharper spur?
Hath love in thy old blood no living fire?
Edward's seven sons, whereof thyself art one,
Were—as seven phials of his sacred blood,
Or seven fair branches springing from one root;
Some of those seven are dried by nature's course,
Some of those branches by the destinies cut :
But Thomas, my dear lord, my life, my Gloster,—
One phial full of Edward's sacred blood,
One flourishing branch of his most royal root,—
Is crack'd, and all the precious liquor spilt;
Is hack'd down, and his summer leaves all faded,
By envy's hand, and murder's bloody axe.

In the following illustration the mind is first occupied with the metaphor "There is a tide," by which he intends depicting the fortunate turning-point of man's career; a pause, and then the literal—"in the affairs of men" (a break in the thought, which, of course, requires a pause); then the metaphor is again taken up and held uninterruptedly to the close; human life is here supposed to be a "voyage at sea."

> *Bru.* Under your pardon.—You must note beside,
> That we have tried the utmost of our friends,
> Our legions are brim-ful, our cause is ripe:
> The enemy increaseth every day;
> We, at the height, are ready to decline.
> There is a tide—in the affairs of men,—
> Which, taken at the flood, leads on to fortune;
> Omitted, all the voyage of their life
> Is bound in shallows, and in miseries.
> On such a full sea are we now afloat;
> And we must take the current when it serves,
> Or lose our ventures.
> —*Julius Cæsar, Act* 4, *Sc.* 3.

The next is from Fingal; I have placed a little dash between the literal and metaphorical to mark the pause.

"Blessed be thy soul, thou king of shells! said Swaran of the dark-brown shield. In peace thou art—the gale of spring; in war—the mountain storm. Take now my hand in friendship, thou noble king of Morven!"

In the following lines the literal thought stops after "state of man"; the metaphor is then carried on, until the word "falls" has been pronounced, when the thought breaks, and the literal is resumed on "as I do."

> *Wol.* So farewell to the little good you bear me.
> Farewell, a long farewell, to all my greatness!

This is the state of man ;—to-day he puts forth
The tender leaves of hope, to-morrow blossoms,
And bears his blushing honors thick upon him :
The third day, comes a frost, a killing frost ;
And (when he thinks, good easy man, full surely
His greatness is a ripening) nips his root,
And then he falls,—as I do. I have ventured,
Like little wanton boys that swim on bladders,
This many summers in a sea of glory ;
But far beyond my depth : my high-blown pride
At length broke under me ; and now has left me,
Weary, and old with service, to the mercy
Of a rude stream, that must for ever hide me.
Vain pomp, and glory of this world, I hate ye ;
I feel my heart new opened : O, how wretched
Is that poor man, that hangs on princes' favors !
There is, betwixt that smile we would aspire to,
That sweet aspect of princes, and their ruin,
More pangs and fears than wars or women have ;
And when he falls, he falls [like Lucifer],
Never to hope again.
—*Henry VIII.*

§ 4.—WONDER. THE MARVELLOUS.

These we express by retarded time. If the reader will take the trouble to notice the "time" in which those around him speak when under the influence of wonder, or in relating that which they consider a marvel, he will perceive that this is a natural law. If this be so, as it undoubtedly is, then is it natural and proper to read all passages of this nature,—miraculous occurrences, fulfillment of prophecy, etc., etc.,— in "time" which, as the reader or speaker goes on, becomes slower, and yet slower.

Take the following example of "wonder" from Matt. 9 : 8; I have given the seven preceding verses because of their containing illustrations of the quotation, given slowly, and with disparagement. The *retarded* time begins with the 8th verse, the intervals of time between the words becoming longer and longer. When a passage has been selected for practice of the "retarded time," the student will graduate the intervals most carefully; and accustom himself to expressing a greater or lesser degree of wonder, according to the time in which he commences the passage; and the degree of wonder to be expressed should determine that.

1 And he entered into a ship, and passed over, and came into his own city.

2 And, behold, they brought to him a man sick of the palsy, lying on a bed : and Jesus seing their faith said unto the sick of the palsy : "Son, be of good cheer; thy sins be forgiven thee."

3 And, behold, certain of the scribes said within themselves, "This man blasphemeth."

4 And Jesus knowing their thoughts said, "Wherefore think ye evil in your hearts ? "

5 For whether is easier, to say, "Thy sins be forgiven thee ;" or to say, "Arise, and walk?"

6 But that ye may know that the Son of man hath power on earth to forgive sins, (then saith he to the sick of the palsy,) "Arise, take up thy bed, and go unto thine house."

7 And he arose, and departed to his house.

8 But when the multitudes saw it, they marvelled, and glorified God, which had given such power unto men.

The next illustration records a miracle; it is from the same chapter; in the 25th verse the miraculous occurrence is related:

23 And when Jesus came into the ruler's house, and saw the minstrels and the people making a noise,

24 He said unto them, "Give place: for the maid is not dead, but sleepeth." And they laughed him to scorn.

Retarded Time.

25 But when the people were put forth, he went in, and took her by the hand, and the maid arose.

26 And the fame hereof went abroad into all that land.

In the first ten verses of the 37th chapter of Ezekiel, we have fulfillment of prophecy. In the 3d, 4th, and 5th verses there are examples of the slow quotation:

Ordinary Time.

1 The hand of the Lord was upon me, and carried me out in the Spirit of the Lord, and set me down in the midst of the valley which was full of bones,

2 And caused me to pass by them round about: and, behold, there were very many in the open valley; and, lo, they were very dry.

Slow Quotation.

3 And he said unto me: "Son of man, can these bones live?" And I answered, "O Lord God, thou knowest."

4 Again he said unto me, "Prophesy upon these bones, and say unto them, O ye dry bones, hear the word of the Lord."

Slow Quotation.

5 Thus saith the Lord God unto these bones: "Behold, I will cause breath to enter into you, and ye shall live:

6 And I will lay sinews upon you, and will bring up flesh upon you, and cover you with skin, and put breath in you, and ye shall live; and ye shall *know* that I am the Lord."

Retarded Time.

7 So I prophesied as I was commanded: ‖and as I prophesied, there was a noise, and behold a shaking, and the bones came together, bone to his bone.

8 And when I beheld, lo, the sinews and the flesh came up upon them, and the skin covered them above: ‖but there was no breath in them.

Ordinary Time.

9 Then said he unto me, Prophesy unto the wind, prophesy, son of man, and say to the wind, Thus saith the Lord God: "Come from the four winds, O breath, and breathe upon these slain, that they may live."

Retarded Time.

10 So I prophesied as he commanded me, ‖and the breath came into them, and they lived, and stood up upon their feet, an exceeding great army.

I have placed a short perpendicular mark at the beginning of the lines requiring the retarded time; also at the points where ordinary time is resumed.

§ 5.—PARABLES.

The parable should, as a whole, be read in faster time than the main text, as it is an illustration, and not of so much importance as the subject it illustrates. That which is of greater moment is the teaching or moral that the parable is intended to point; and the teaching, consequently, must be rendered very much more slowly than either main text or parable.

I append an example from St. Luke.

12 He said therefore,—A certain nobleman went into a far country to receive for himself a kingdom, and to return.

13 And he called his ten servants, and delivered them ten pounds, and said unto them, Occupy till I come.

14 But his citizens hated him, and sent a message after him, saying, We will not have this man to reign over us.

15 And it came to pass, that when he was returned, having received the kingdom, then he commanded these servants to be called unto him, to whom he had given the money, that he might know how much every man had gained by trading.

16 Then came the first, saying, Lord, thy pound hath gained ten pounds.

17 And he said unto him, Well, thou good servant: because thou hast been faithful in a very little, have thou authority over ten cities.

18 And the second came, saying, Lord, thy pound hath gained five pounds.

19 And he said likewise to him, Be thou also over five cities.

20 And another came, saying, Lord, behold, here is thy pound, which I have kept laid up in a napkin:

21 For I feared thee, because thou art an austere man: thou takest up that thou layedst not down, and reapest that thou didst not sow.

22 And he saith unto him, "Out of thine own mouth will I judge thee, thou wicked servant. Thou knewest that I was an austere man, taking up that I laid not down, and reaping that I did not sow:

23 Wherefore then gavest not thou my money into the bank, that at my coming I might have required mine own with usury?

24 And he said unto them that stood by, "Take from him the pound, and give it to him that hath ten pounds."

25 (And they said unto him, Lord, he hath ten pounds.)

Teaching.

26 For I say unto you, That unto every one which hath shall be given; and from him that hath not, even that he hath shall be taken away from him.

For a second illustration I give the parable of "The sower and the seed," from Matthew, chap. 13:

1 The same day went Jesus out of the house, and sat by the sea-side.

2 And great multitudes were gathered together unto him, so that he went into a ship and sat; and the whole multitude stood on the shore.

3 And he spake many things unto them in parables, saying, Behold, a sower went forth to sow;

4 And when he sowed, some seeds fell by the way side, and the fowls came and devoured them up:

5 Some fell upon stony places, where they had not much earth: and forthwith they sprung up, because they had no deepness of earth:

6 And when the sun was up, they were scorched; and because they had no root, they withered away.

7 And some fell among thorns; and the thorns sprung up, and choked them:

8 But other fell into good ground, and brought forth fruit, some an hundredfold, some sixtyfold, some thirtyfold.

Teaching—"Now the 'seed' is the word of God," etc.

CHAPTER III.

EMPHASIS.

§ 1.—ITS PHILOSOPHY AND PRACTICAL EXECUTION.

CERTAIN dynamic or creative acts of the mind result in the vocal phenomena which we call "emphasis." A new idea or fact, one now presented for the first time, constitutes the emphatic word or words. The dominant idea in a passage is the fact which requires prominence. These successive new facts (or ideas) form as it were a chain; each emphatic word or clause forms a "link" of different pattern or weight perhaps, but wrought into one connected and harmonious whole. As the missing or losing of one of its links would be fatal to the perfection of the chain, so the suppression of even one of the emphatic words or clauses in a sentence is most detrimental to its force and clearness. It follows from this that the "unemphatic clause" must be that which presents no new or dominant fact or thought; and although these unemphatic clauses occur very frequently, their features are so plainly marked as always to give us fair warning not to give them undue prominence; this latter being a fault which is the cause of apparent "weakness" in many passages, that properly rendered would carry great weight with them.

The "characteristics" that mark the "unemphatic clause" are principally these—1. *Repetition;* 2. *Anticipation;* 3. *Sequence;* 4. *Subordination;* 5. *Knowledge beforehand.*

Repetition of an idea that has already been presented is illustrated in the 1st, 2d, 3d, 4th, and 11th verses of the 5th chapter of Daniel.

1 Belshazzar the king made a great feast to a thousand of his lords, and drank wine before the thousand.

2 Belshazzar, while he tasted the wine, commanded to bring the golden and silver vessels which his father Nebuchadnezzar had taken out of the temple which was in Jerusalem; that the king and his princes, his wives and his concubines, might drink therein.

3 Then they brought the golden vessels that were taken out of the temple of the house of God which was at Jerusalem; and the king and his princes, his wives and his concubines, drank in them.

4 They drank wine, and praised the gods of gold, and of silver, of brass, of iron, of wood, and of stone.

"Belshazzar" is the first emphatic word; "the king" is a repetition of Belshazzar; it is therefore unemphatic; also, on pronouncing "Belshazzar" we anticipate that it is the king of that name of whom we are speaking, consequently "the king" is unemphatic through "anticipation" as well as "repetition"; "great feast" is the next new fact stated, and is consequently emphatic; "to a thousand of his lords" is a clause unemphatic through both anticipation and sequence; for, if the king made a great feast, we anticipate that it was for a great number; it is unemphatic through sequence, for as a natural consequence of the preparation of a "great feast" many are expected to partake, and the exact number, whether 999 or a thousand, is not of the slightest importance; "drank wine" is the next new fact, and "before the thousand" is unemphatic through "repetition" of an idea that has already been presented.

The student will proceed in like manner when analyzing the succeeding verses. In the 2d verse the new facts are—"Belshazzar" "commanded to bring the golden and silver vessels" "which his father" "had taken out of the temple"; and in the last part of the verse the various nouns "king," "princes," "wives," "concubines" merely represent the pronominal "they," —so that after emphasizing "king" the rest are unemphatic through repetition, anticipation, or sequence. "Therein" is the next emphatic word; "drank" being a repeated fact, the new idea being that the company should drink "*from*" these sacred vessels. "While he tasted the wine" is unemphatic through "repetition"; "Nebuchadnezzar," a repetition of "father"; "which was in Jerusalem," unemphatic through "sequence" and through "knowledge beforehand" (we know that the sacred vessels were in the temple there).

In the third verse the only new ideas are conveyed in the words "brought" and "drank," each telling of an accomplished fact; the remainder of the verse is plainly unemphatic through "repetition."

"And praised the gods of gold," is the only new fact stated in the fourth verse. After drinking from the sacred vessels (which we have heard they did), they commit *idolatry;* that fact is stated by emphasizing "*and praised the gods of gold;*" we anticipate that they did not confine themselves to one particular metal, and we conclude, as a natural consequence of their falling into idolatry, and praising the gods of gold, that they praised those of silver, etc., also.

A peculiarity which commands our attention in the fifth verse, is the concentration of the new fact in a single word:

5 In the same hour came forth fingers of a man's hand, and wrote over against the candlestick upon the plaster of the wall of the king's palace: and the king saw the part of the hand that wrote.

The ideas thus outlined are, first, the "*time*," by emphasizing "*same*" (this identical time); next, the *object* "fingers" (not fingers of this or that man or supernatural being); then the *action* "wrote," not the particular spot on which they wrote; we anticipate that they wrote somewhere within full view; the wonder being in supernatural writing, not in the particular angle of wall chosen to receive it. There is nothing new in the candlestick or wall, but only in the marvelous fact that strange fingers appeared writing mysterious words. Lastly, the king "*saw*"; emphasis on this word implies not only the king's actual perceiving what was done, but also the effect it had upon him; that of alarm, or interest, as the case may be. The unemphatic clauses "of a man's hand" and "over against a candlestick upon the plaster of the wall of the king's palace," are so through both sequence and anticipation. To emphasize "the part of the hand that wrote" would be incorrect, first through "repetition" (that was the only part that appeared), then these words are simply equivalent to the pronoun "it"; and so much of this kind of repetition abounds that we might designate this description of unemphatic clause, "Pronominal repetition."

In the eleventh verse of this chapter—

There is a man in thy kingdom, in whom is the spirit of the holy gods; and in the days of thy father light and understanding and wisdom, like the wisdom of the gods, was found in him; whom the king Nebuchadnezzar thy father, the king, I say, thy father, made master of the magicians, astrologers, Chaldeans, and soothsayers;—

occurs an example of words or clauses unemphatic through "subordination," the rule being that when two words, etc., in connection are each repeated, it is for the purpose of making each emphatic in turn, and that the *second* word is subordinate to the *first* in the first place, and the first word is subordinate to the second word in the second place. In this example, "king" is first emphatic (Nebuchadnezzar is a repetition of king), and father is subordinate to king; then, in the second place, "father" is emphatic, and king is subordinate.

"When should a repeated word be emphasized?"
"When it has a new signification."

We have, in the previous examples, dealt with sentences in which the repeated word has given us no *new* idea, but we meet with it where it has a new meaning; in such cases it has all the logical power of a new word. Some illustrations will be the best explanation of this natural principle:

For he that is entered into his rest, he also hath ceased from [*his own*] works, as God did from *his*.—*Hebrews* 4 : 10.

"His own," in the second line, is massed and emphatic, "his" referring to man; the last "his" is also given with force, because of its different meaning—it refers to God.

In 1 Cor. 15 : 21—

"For since by m$\overset{\frown}{a}$n came death, by m$\overset{\frown}{a}$n came also the *resurrection* of the dead "—

the repeated word "man," signifying the Son of God, requires as much emphasis as does the first man, referring to Adam; though with regard to the first man (Adam) we have the negative attitude of mind (⌒), and the "positive" (⌢) as to Christ.

The following example is from 1 Kings, ch. 18 :

6 So they divided the land between them to pass throughout it : Ahab went one way by *himself*, and Obadiah went another way by *him*self.

Although the repeated word "himself" has a new signification, the first referring to Ahab, the second to Obadiah, both requiring emphasis; the "ear" is so nice in its distinctions that where there is a possibility of "transfer" it will detect it, and in this instance, after the usual emphasis has been given to the first of these words, with the stress upon the last syllable "self," in giving the repeated emphasis to the second word, the transfer of the "stress" to "*him*" is both easy and natural.

In the following example the same transfer of stress indicates that the first "*over*come" is passive, the second "over*come*" active:

Be not *over*come of *evil*, but over*come* evil with *good*. —*Romans* 12 : 21.

Day unto *day* uttereth speech, and *night* unto *night* sheweth knowledge.—*Psalm* 19 : 2.

The second "day" should be as emphatic as the first "day"; it is not the same but a different day that is meant. So with the word "*night*," each is emphatic for the same reason.

§ 2.—MASSING.

This is a deeply interesting feature of emphasis; it consists of an accumulation of successive particulars, words or clauses, which should be given as a unit with one impetus. There are many and varied instances, in which the employment of massing is necessary, and although these may require somewhat different modes of execution, all have their mental origin as a "unit," and the delivery should indicate this singleness of feature which characterizes them. Thus in one case it may be an abstract quality or idea, as the *omniscience* of God:

For the [word of God] [is quick, and powerful, and sharper than any two-edged sword, piercing even to the dividing asunder of soul and spirit, and of the joints and marrow, and is a discerner of the thoughts and intents of the heart].

Neither is there any creature that is not manifest in his sight; but all things [are naked and opened unto the eyes of him with whom we have to do].—*Hebrews* 4 : 12, 13.

Or of "universality":

And his fame went throughout all Syria; and they brought unto him [all sick people that were taken with divers diseases and torments, and those which were possessed with devils, and those which were lunatick, and those that had the palsy] ; and he healed them.—*Matt.* 4 : 21.

These examples are marked by placing a small bracket just above the beginning of the first word introducing the massed clauses, and another at their termination.

Massed words or clauses may be of "identity," as found in various parts of the fifth chapter of Daniel:

"[Peoples, nations, and languages]."
"[Light, understanding, and wisdom]."
"[Astrologers, Chaldeans, and soothsayers]."

"Then was king Belshazzar greatly troubled : [and his countenance was changed in him, and his lords were astonished]."

Ezekiel 22 : 20 :

19 Therefore thus saith the Lord God: As I live, surely mine oath that he hath despised, and my covenant that he hath broken, even it will I recompense upon his own head.

20 [And I will spread my net upon him, and he shall be taken in my snare, and I will bring him to Babylon, and will plead with him there for his trespass that he hath trespassed against me.

21 And all his fugitives with all his bands shall fall by the sword, and they that remain shall be scattered toward all winds:] and ye shall know that I the Lord have spoken it.

The several particulars mentioned from the beginning of the 20th verse through the word "winds" in the 21st verse, all refer to the "recompense," *are* in fact the recompense; they should then be read as *one* idea, and not as several.

In Ezekiel 18 : 20, I see a similar example of massing the several clauses, beginning "the son shall not bear, etc.," all referring to the fact that each is accountable for his own sins :

The soul that sinneth, it shall die. [The son shall not bear the iniquity of the father, neither shall the father bear the iniquity of the son: the righteousness of the righteous shall be upon him, and the wickedness of the wicked shall be upon *him.*]

In Luke 24 : 25—

"Then he said unto them, "O fools, and [slów of héart to *believe*] all the prophets have spoken"—

the meaning is indicated by massing the words "slów of heart to *believe*" and giving them with the negative inflection of voice, which shows *disapproval;* the words are massed, because they convey but one idea.

§ 3.—EMPHASES BY TRANSFER.

When a word is repeated, "transfer" the emphasis to another word. This is a natural process whenever the sense will admit of it, and it does admit of it whenever the repeated word gives the same meaning as its predecessor.

12 Forasmuch [as an excellent spirit, and knowledge, and understanding, interpreting of dreams, and shewing of hard sentences, and dissolving of doubts,] were found in the same Daniel, whom the king named Belteshazzar: now let Daniel be *called*, and *he* will shew the interpretation.

13 Then was Daniel brought in before the king. And the king spake and said unto Daniel, Art thou that Daniel, which art of the children of the captivity of Judah, whom the king my father brought out of Jewry?

14 I have even heard of thee, that the spirit of the gods is in thee, and that light and understanding and excellent wisdom is found in thee.

15 And now the wise men, the astrologers, have been

brought in before me, that they should read this writing, and make known unto me the interpretation thereof: but they could not shew the interpretation of the thing:

16 And I have heard of thee, that thou canst make interpretations, and dissolve doubts: now if thou canst read the writing, and make known to me the interpretation thereof, thou shalt be clothed with scarlet, and have a chain of gold about thy neck, and shalt be the third ruler in the kingdom.

17 Then Daniel answered and said before the king, Let thy gifts be to thyself, and give thy rewards to another; yet I will read the writing unto the king, and make known to him the interpretation.

18 O thou king, the most high God gave Nebuchadnezzar thy father a kingdom, and majesty, and glory, and honour:

19 And for the majesty that he gave him, all people, nations, and languages, trembled and feared before him: whom he would he slew; and whom he would he kept alive; and whom he would he set up; and whom he would he put down.

Let us analyze the above verses (from Daniel, ch. 5), not confining ourselves to the examples of "transfer" only, but taking all that are involved in each verse, beginning with the 12th. "Forasmuch as an excellent spirit, and knowledge, and understanding, interpreting of dreams, and shewing of hard sentences, and dissolving of doubts," all refer to one thought, that of surpassing wisdom; the several clauses should therefore be presented as a *unit*, that is, without any special pausing between them. "Were found in the same Daniel" is a clause unemphatic through *anticipation.* "Whom the king named Belteshazzar" is an unimportant parenthesis. As Daniel has been spoken of all along, instead of repeating the emphasis upon Daniel in the next clause, *transfer* it to "*called,*" which conveys to us the next new thought, and from "interpretation," which we have had before, to "he." "Brought in" is the first new fact in the 13th verse; "spake" is next emphatic; "and said unto Daniel," unemphatic through repetition. Now follows a sentence in the interrogative *form*, but the *spirit* of which is certainly assertive, as the king's subsequent words prove; for he goes on to say, "I have even *heard* of thee that the [spirit of the gods] (massed), is in thee, and that light, and understanding, and excellent wisdom is found in thee.". (It will be correct either to *mass* these last, or to consider that the idea is fully given in the word "light," and that the other qualities are unemphatic through *Sequence.*) The sentence spoken of as being assertive, though interrogative in form, is treated of at length in the section on *Antagonism of Grammatical Forms.* "Is found in thee" is unemphatic through "*anticipation.*" In the 15th verse, "And now the wise men" (emphatic); "the astrologers" (unemphatic through repetition); "read" (emphatic). "Interpretation" is the next new fact, (to *Daniel*, for Daniel has not known of this before, and although it is not new to those who have been present all the time, it is new to Daniel.) The next new idea is contained in the negative; and that word alone requires emphasis—"But they could NOT show the interpretation of the thing." 16th verse—"And I have heard of thee that *thou* (transfer the emphasis from *thee* to *thou*) canst make interpretations, and dissolve doubts (unemphatic through repetition); now if thou canst (transfer the emphasis from *thou* to *canst*) read the writing and make known to me the interpretation thereof (unemphatic through repetition), thou shalt be clothed (unemphatic through Sequence) with scarlet (a new fact, an honor, therefore emphatic), and have a chain of gold (emphatic, the new fact, the honor) about thy neck (unemphatic through *Anticipation*), and shalt be the third ruler (emphatic) in the kingdom" (unemphatic through sequence or anticipation).

17th verse. "Then Daniel answered" (emphatic) "and said before the king" (unemphatic through repetition). "Thyself," "another," "read," and "known" are the remaining emphatic words in the slow quotation as far as the end of the verse; this quotation is, however, continued in the following verses.

18th verse. "O thou king, the most high God gave Nebuchadnezzar (emphatic) thy father" (unemphatic through both repetition and anticipation). "Kingdom," "majesty," "glory," "honor," are each emphatic in turn, as they are each different, and the gift of one of these does not presuppose any of the others. This may be called the converse of massing.

19th verse. The first line is unemphatic as far as "people." "Nations and languages" must either be massed with people or be considered unemphatic, because they repeat the idea given in the word "people"; "*trembled*" is the next emphatic word; "feared" is unemphatic through anticipation; if they trembled, we anticipate that fear was the emotional cause. Now we have a certain amount of repetition, and admitting that "transfer" is pleasing for the *variety* it imparts, we will find better reasons for its employ in the following lines.

"Whom he would he slew." *Slew* should be emphatic, and in tone negative (that is, with the rising inflection); and the next new fact is conveyed in the word "*alive*," which is emphatic, and in tone *positive* (or with the falling inflection of voice—reasons given under the section, *Positive and Negative Inflections*). Transfer the emphasis to "*whom*" for this reason: whomsoever the person was, no matter *how* poor or lowly, he was able to elevate him ; transfer the emphasis, therefore, from "whom" to "*would*," for the reason that it was immaterial to him how high or mighty a man might be, if he *willed* it or *would*, he could put him down.

In Isaiah 55 : 1, we find an example of transfer; the "new idea" is found in a new word and not in the repeated words, of which there are a great many. The words requiring emphasis are "thirsteth," "come," "waters," "money," "buy," "wine," "without," and "price":

Ho, every one that *thirsteth, come* ye to the waters, and he that hath no *money ;* come ye, *buy*, and eat ; yea, come, buy *wine* and milk *without* money and without *price*.

The new thoughts in the following example are made prominent by transferring the emphasis as indicated:

8 For though I made you *sorry* with a letter, I do not *repent*, though I *did* repent : for I *perceive* that the same epistle hath made you sorry, though it were but for a *season*.

9 Now I *rejoice*, (not that ye were made sorry,) but that ye sorrowed to *repentance:* for ye were made sorry after a *godly* manner, that ye might receive damage by us in *nothing*.

10 For godly sorrow worketh [repentance to *salvation*] not to be repented of : but the [sorrow of the world] worketh *death*.

11 [For behold this selfsame thing, that ye sorrowed after a godly sort], what *carefulness* it wrought in you, yea, what *clearing* of yourselves, yea, what *indignation*, yea, what *fear*, yea, what vehement *desire*, yea, what *zeal*, yea, what *revenge!* In all things ye have approved yourselves to be *clear* in this matter.

12 Wherefore, though I wrote unto you, I did it not for his cause that had *done* the wrong, nor for his cause that *suffered* wrong, but that our *care* for you in the sight of God might *appear* unto you.—2 *Cor.*, ch. 7.

The massed clauses are enclosed (partially) by small brackets; the negative attitude of mind with regard to certain thoughts by the negative inflection (´)

above the words so regarded, whether they be emphatic or not, and the positive attitude of mind as indicated by placing the positive or downward inflection (\) over certain other words expressive of thoughts of a positive nature. All words that are emphatic are in italics.

"In the beginning was the word, and the word was with God, and the word was God."

In John 1 : 1, the dominant thought (Christ's divinity) is brought out clearly and concisely by emphasizing first "*beginning*"; the first thought being that Christ *always* was. Transfer the emphasis to "*God*," to show that Christ was not only from the beginning but that he was always God; and now transfer the emphasis to "*Word*," which brings to the mind's eye forcibly that the *Word* was not only with *God* but that the WORD was God; do not emphasize "was"—the weakly false emphasis that many give—by that you not only suppress the dominant idea that the "*Word*" was God, but raise in the mind unnecessary doubts, as "He was, but is He now? and will He be?" exploring little byroads in the analysis that are irrelevant, and forsaking the broad road where lies the dominant thought. A good rule to follow, in order to avoid such divergence, is this: Read "ideas" instead of "words."

In 1 Kings 18 : 21—

"If the Lord be God follow him, but if Baal then follow him "—

we have both "follow" and "him" repeated. What is the speaker's own belief? Why, that the "*Lord*" is God; then his positive attitude of mind as regards the Lord, requires the positive inflection of voice (\) on that word; it is the first new thought, and requires emphasis in consequence. "*Follow*" is the next new idea; then transfer the force to "*Baal*," whom the speaker does not believe to be God, so holds a negative attitude of mind with regard to him, which he shows by the negative inflection of voice; afterwards comes the word "*him*," to which the emphasis is transferred.

In the following example from Matt. 10 : 34—

"Think not that I am come to send peace on earth : I came not to send peace, but a *sword*"—

the new thought is made prominent by emphasizing "*peace*"; the idea next put forward is contained in the word which conveys the idea of what he did come for, viz., to send a "*sword*"; the mental attitude is indicated by the inflections as placed. The transfer is from "peace" to "sword."

Referring to the parable of the "Prodigal Son," we find that "he" has been applied to the prodigal until we reach the word "*citizen*," which is emphatic, but "he" has been transferred from "younger son" to "citizen" we find when we glance at the "he" which follows citizen; then should the emphasis be transferred also.

And when he had spent all, there arose a mighty famine in that land ; and he began to be in want.

And he went and joined himself to a citizen of that country ; and *he* sent him into his fields to feed swine.—*Luke* 15 : 14, 15.

An excellent example of transfer is found in Hebrews 2 : 6, 8 :

6 But one in a certain place testified, saying, What is *man*, that thou art *mindful* of him ? or the *son* of man, that thou *visitest* him ?

*　　*　　*　　*　　*　　*

8 Thou hast put all things in *subjection* under his feet. For in that he put *all* in subjection under him, he left *nothing* that is not put under him. But now we *see* not yet all things put under him.

We have here a "slow quotation"; the emphasis is first on "man," then upon "mindful"; then transfer the force to "son," and finally to "visitest." By transferring the force in this way, in the eighth verse, each *new* thought is brought out in sharp and perfect outline—a word more or a word less than is absolutely necessary in the emphasis renders the idea you wish to define obscure. The thoughts in this verse are clearly brought out by emphasizing successively "subjection," "all," "nothing," "see." Ideas are thus put forward without explanation and embellishment.

The rule in this matter of transfer is: In all repetitions of the same word, in an identical sense, transfer the emphasis to another word.

§ 4.—MENTAL PROJECTION.

When in the utterance of one clause the mind is already engaged with the succeeding one, the process is termed "mental projection"; and the latter clause is denominated "a clause unemphatic through mental projection"; because in the act of uttering the first clause the mind is employed with what is to follow, and persons listening surmise instantaneously what is to come. As an illustration—in Julius Cæsar, Act 1, Sc. 2, Cassius says:

"What is there in this same Cæsar," etc.

" Write them together, yours is as fair a name,
Sound them it doth become the mouth as well,
Weigh them it is as heavy ; conjure with them
Brutus will start a spirit as soon as Cæsar."

Cassius, in uttering "Write them together," must be *thinking* of what he is next to say, and the mind of his auditor naturally reverts to the implied sequence, that one name looks as well as the other. So with the succeeding clauses: when Cassius says, "Sound them," the next words are immediately mentally projected; when he says, "Weigh them," you know what will follow. And that there is no more of magic in one name than in the other you conceive the instant that Cassius says, "Conjure with them." These clauses then are unemphatic through having been mentally projected before they were uttered in so many words.

Another example of the "clause unemphatic through mental projection" we take from Matt. 5 : 34, 35, 36 :

33 Again, ye have heard that it hath been said by them of old time, "Thou shalt not forswear thyself, but shalt perform unto the Lord thine oaths :"
34 But I say unto you, Swear not at all ; neither by heaven ; for it is God's throne :
35 Nor by the earth ; for it is his footstool : neither by Jerusalem ; for it is the city of the great King.
36 Neither shalt thou swear by thy head, because thou canst not make one hair white or black.

The 33d verse contains a quotation rendered with disparagement; then comes the slower time on "Swear not at all; neither by heaven," and while uttering the words "neither by heaven" the mind is naturally employed in thinking of the *reason* for not swearing by heaven—both speaker's and listener's minds revert at once to the *sanctity* of heaven as being the reason; then has the clause, "for it is God's throne," been mentally projected, while pronouncing the words "neither by heaven." The 35th and 36th verses are analyzed in exactly the same manner: "Nor by the earth" (emphatic); "for it is his footstool" (unemphatic through mental projection): "neither by Jerusalem" (emphatic); "for it is the city of the great King" (mentally projected). "Neither shalt thou swear by thy head" (emphatic), "because thou canst not make one hair white or black" (mentally projected).

The next example, besides the clauses unemphatic through mental projection, embraces a quotation of disparagement, and one that is approbatory:

43 Ye have heard that it hath been said, Thou shalt love thy neighbour, and hate thine enemy.
44 But I say unto you, Love your enemies, bless them that curse you, do good to them that hate you, and pray for them which despitefully use you, and persecute you;
45 That ye may be the children of your Father which is in heaven.

In uttering the words that immediately follow the quotation of disparagement, "But I say unto you, Love," the mind at once flies to the opposite of the maxims inculcated in the quotation of disparagement; love what then? "your enemies," "bless (emphatic) them that curse you" (unemphatic, mentally projected), "do good (emphatic) to them that hate you" (unemphatic, m. p.), "and pray (emphatic) for them which despitefully use you, and persecute you" (unem.). "That ye may be the children of your Father which is in heaven" (emphatic).

Another example is found in Matt. 7 : 7, 8 :

7 Ask, and it shall be given you; seek, and ye shall find; knock, and it shall be opened unto you:
8 For every one that asketh receiveth; and he that seeketh findeth; and to him that knocketh it shall be opened.

The emphatic words (or new facts stated) being

"ask," "seek," "knock"; the other clauses in that verse are mentally projected by each of those words successively. "Receiveth," "findeth," "it shall be opened" (in the 8th verse) are mentally projected by the clauses that immediately precede them.

The next examples are from the 24th and 25th verses of Matt. 7:

24 * * * I will liken him unto a wise man which built his house upon a rock:

25 And the rain descended, and the floods came, and the winds blew, and beat upon that house,—

is an example of massing, the several clauses presenting one and the same idea—that of violent assault from the elements; and in the utterance of that idea, the faculties must necessarily be engaged with the consequences of such an attack upon the house with so sure a foundation; then is mentally projected the clause, "and it fell not, for it was founded upon a rock."

In Romans 12 : 19, we find an example of the slow quotation; it is given here because of its fitness in introducing the 20th verse containing clauses mentally projected, they being "feed him," and "give him drink." The break in the thought between the literal and metaphorical occurs after the word "shalt," the metaphor then begins.*

-* This metaphor is supposed to be taken from the melting of metals, by covering the ore with burning coals; the meaning, "In so doing, thou wilt mollify thine enemy and bring him to feel kindly," etc.

19 Dearly beloved, avenge not yourselves, but rather give place unto wrath: for it is written, Vengeance is mine; I will repay, saith the Lord.

20 Therefore if thine enemy hunger, feed him; if he thirst, give him drink: for in so doing thou shalt heap coals of fire on his head.

CHAPTER IV.

INFLECTION.

§ 1.—GENERAL PRINCIPLES.

INFLECTIONS of voice indicate the true place and standpoint of each thought;—the mental attitude regarding certain facts or ideas; the negative or positive light in which the mind views them.

Readings, lectures, sermons, etc., are frequently rendered confused and obscure through ignorance of this important principle; sometimes an *opposite* meaning from the one intended is first indicated by the voice, and then accepted by the mind. So unerring is the human ear in detecting meaning, even *shades* of meaning, by tones when they are natural (or true), that, without having caught the words, or been present to observe looks or gestures, people say, "from the sounds I judged that some one was angry;" or "that there was a quarrel, or that some one was advocating a certain measure" or "course of conduct," or from their voices I surmised that one was mercilessly condemning, the other was imploring leniency, or pardon, or grace, or whatnot." Why are we not as instantaneously convinced of the lecturer's or reader's intention? Why is not the preacher's meaning equally evident? It is because few of these people have studied what they and all of us do *naturally* under given circumstances, or conditions of feeling; they have never observed the natural process of interpreting certain attitudes of the mind, consequently have no fixed principles on which to base their manner of interpreting any given idea.

The positive and negative inflections of voice are antithetic, but these inflections, psychologically applied, cover a far wider area of "thought" than has ever been accorded to antithesis. The "positive attitude" is indicated by the downward inflection (\) or circumflex (⌢), which last is a combination of the upward (/) and downward (\) inflections. The "negative attitude" is expressed by the upward inflection (/) or circumflex (⌣), which is a combination of the downward (\) and upward (/) inflections. If any one will observe closely the inflections of voice that others use in an unstudied, unpremeditated way, he will perceive that what the speaker wishes to endorse, or to advocate, etc., will be spoken in positive tones; that is, the voice takes a downward turn on each of the principal words in such advocated thought or idea. Beginning on a certain key (in pronouncing the word to be rendered positively), the voice travels in an inclined direction downward, and the word is finished on a lower key than the one on which it was commenced. Does the speaker desire to describe certain facts as unfavorable, certain ideas as injurious, etc., his voice will naturally rise (/) on the principal words; by which upward turn of voice he indicates the "*negative attitude*" of mind.

The reader will bear in mind that the rule for his guidance in this matter is that—The *main* purpose of the speaker (or supposed speaker), or author, is always *positive*. The inflections of voice must be sufficiently *marked* to express the negative and positive intentions.

A few examples of words, the signification of which is invariable, arranged in their respective classes of positives and negatives, may be useful. The few here mentioned are intended to serve merely as a guide:

Positive ＼.	*Negative* ／.
Certain.	Uncertain.
Good.	Bad.
Present.	Past.
Right.	Wrong.
Benefit.	Injury.
Favorable.	Unfavorable.
Absolute.	Conditional.
Peace.	War.
Plenty.	Famine.
Sunshine.	Storm.

If it be the author's or the speaker's *purpose* to *advocate* or *endorse* any thought, feeling, or fact, which as a general thing would be viewed from a negative standpoint, then has the mental attitude towards that thought or fact become "positive," and should be rendered with the downward inflection (＼). When it is the speaker's intention to denounce wrong or evil, his words of denouncement take the positive inflection of voice.

The circumflex ⌢ ⌣ is of service when the ordinary inflections (╲ ╱) are not considered powerful enough to express the required degree of positive or negative force.

We give some examples illustrative of these principles. From Julius Cæsar, Act 3, Scene 2:

I come to bury Cæsar, not to praise him."

"The evil that men do, lives after them; the good is oft interred with their bones."

"Evil" is strongly negative; that it should be remembered of its perpetrators is no more than they deserve —positive. "Good"—positive—is forgotten; a subject of regret, therefore negative; the downward turn of voice, indicated after the negative circumflex on "bones," merely points to the natural cadence or fall of the voice at the termination of the sentence.

"Sink or swim, live or die, survive or perish, I give my hand and my heart to this vote."

"Think not that I am come to send *peace* on earth: I come not to send peace—but a *sword*."—*Matt.* 10:34.

ANALYSIS.—Peace, as a general thing, is viewed positively; it is under most circumstances preferable to the sword; yet here the speaker endorses "war," and this is indicated by rendering "*sword*" with the positive inflection.

Macbeth, Act 2, Scene 3:

Macb. Who can be wise, amazed, temperate, and furious,
Loyal and neutral, [in a moment]? No man:

ANALYSIS.—If he were amazed and furious at sight of Duncan's murder, how could you expect him to be at the same time wise and temperate, the antipodes of the former moods? If he were loyal to Duncan, how could he be expected to take a neutral course!

2 Cor. 3 : 5, 6 :

5 Not that we are sufficient of ourselves to [think any thing] as of ourselves; but our sufficiency is of *God;*

6 Who also hath made us [*able* ministers] of the new testament; not of the letter, but of the *spirit:* for the letter killeth, but the spirit giveth *life.*

ANALYSIS.—That we may value our abilities (*think* any thing—positive), but, not as originating in ourselves, but in *God.* "Who also hath made us able ministers" (pos.), "not of the letter (neg.) but of the spirit" (pos.), not of preaching only, but of practice, not of the mere words, but of the thoughts contained —"letter killeth (neg.), spirit giveth life" (pos.).

Our next example is from York's speech, when, after being taken prisoner, he is railed at by Queen

Margaret; these lines occur in the last portion of his answer to her. Hatred and anger are the dominant passions; the tones which indicate those passions will be found described under the section, "*Symbols of the Passions.*"

York. * * *

Pos. 'Tis *beauty*, that doth oft make women proud;
Neg. But God, he knows, *thy* share thereof is small;
Pos. 'Tis *virtue*, that doth make them most admired;
Neg. The contrary doth make thee wonder'd at;
Pos. 'Tis government, that makes them seem divine;
Neg. The want thereof makes thee abominable;
Neg. Thou art as opposite to every good, (Pos.)
Neg. As the antipodes are unto us, (Pos.)
Neg. Or as the south to the septentrion. (Pos.)
Neg. O [*tiger's* heart], wrapped in a *woman's* hide; (Pos.)
Neg. How couldst thou drain the life-blood of the child;
To bid the father wipe his eyes withal,
And yet be seen to wear a *woman's* face? (Pos.)
Pos. *Women* are *soft*, *mild*, *pitiful*, and *flexible;*
Neg. *Thou* stern, obdurate, flinty, rough, remorseless.

* * * * * *

—*King Henry VI, Part* 3.

The positive and negative intentions are so plainly indicated in the preceding lines that a more lengthy analysis will be unnecessary.

Isabella. "O it is *excellent* to have a [*giant's* strength], but it is tyrannous to *use* it like a giant!"

"*Great* men may jest with *saints:* 'tis *wit* in them;
but in the *less*, foul profanation."—*Measure for Measure.*

In the following lines from Tennyson, the author's meaning is admirably delineated by correct management of the positive and negative inflections; although the sentences are in the interrogative form, they are not so in thought:

"Do we indeed desire the dead
Should still be near us at our side?"

The speaker evidently doubts the desire, consequently views the idea from a negative standpoint; in the next:

"Is there no baseness we would hide,
No inner vileness that we dread?"

It is as evident that the mental attitude is positive, for it is virtually a declaration that because of our baseness and inner vileness we do not desire the dead to be at our side, so should be rendered thus:

"Do we *indeed* desire the dead
Should still be *near* us at our side?
Is there no *baseness* we would hide,
No inner *vileness* that we dread?"

"Tell us, ye dead!
Will none of ye disclose the dreadful secret,
What it is ye *are* and we are *like* to be?"

This last sentence or verse is what is called a "declarative negative," the speaker's thought is that he would like the dead to disclose what it is they are and we are like to be (positive), but that his conviction is that "none" (neg.) will ever do so.

§ 2.—FLUCTUATING INFLECTIONS.

Great interest attends the study of the simple rising and falling inflection, also their combination—the circumflex ⌒ ⌣, over which we have just passed. On turning to the one now presented for our contemplation, the student cannot fail to be delighted with the accuracy of the interpretation, and the promptitude with which it indicates the mind's departure to a new idea, or its divergence from the main track of thought. By the proper application of the fluctuating inflection or "wave," the author's meaning is as clearly evolved as are the different elements in a chemical analysis; yet this delicate instrument (if we may so term it) for conveying "meaning" is seldom or never used by the readers or speakers we are accustomed to hear, unless they extemporize, and then "nature" (if the artificial has not supplanted her) will prompt its due employment.

The "wave" is characteristic of the "illustration"; the "comparison" the "episode";—it enables the *listener* to apprehend that the reader (or speaker) is incidentally departing from his main purpose or topic, and its cessation indicates a return to the main track of thought.

Observe that the "wave" ⌣ ⌒ is nothing like so

pronounced as the circumflex which we use in strong psychological positives and negatives; the wave ‿ ⁀ is as potent in its effects, but of far more delicate calibre. Without this "fluctuating wave" certain portions of the 12th and 14th chapters of the 1st of Corinthians sound precisely as if the language were that of a phrenologist or a professor of physiology addressing a class of students. For example:

1 Now concerning [spiritual gifts], brethren, I would not have you ignorant.

2 Ye know that ye were Gentiles, carried away unto these dumb idols, even as ye were led.

3 Wherefore I give you to understand, that no man speaking by the [Spirit of God] calleth Jesus accursed: and that no man can say that Jesus is the Lord, but by the Holy Ghost.

4 Now there are [*diversities of gifts*], but the [same Spirit].

5 And there are [*differences of administrations*], but the [same Lord].

6 And there are [*diversities of operations*], but it is the [*same* God which worketh all in all].

7 But the [manifestation of the Spirit] is given to every man to profit withal.

8 For to one is given (by the Spirit) the [*word of wisdom*]; to another the [*word of knowledge*] by the [same Spirit];

9 To another [*faith*] by the same Spirit; to another the [gifts of *healing*] by the same Spirit;

10 To another the [working of miracles]; to another [*prophecy*]; to another [discerning of spirits]; to another

[divers kinds of tongues]; to another the [interpretation of tongues]:

11 But all these [worketh that one and the self-same Spirit], dividing to every man severally as he *will*.

12 For as the body is one, and hath many members, and all the members of that one body, being many, are one body: so *also* is *Christ*.

13 For by [one Spirit] are we all baptized into [one body, whether we be Jews or Gentiles, whether we be bond or free; and have been all made to drink into [one Spirit].

14 For the body is not one member, but *many*.

15 If the foot shall say, "Because I am not the hand, I am not of the body"; *is* it therefore not of the body?

16 And if the ear shall say, Because I am not the eye, I am not of the body; is it therefore not of the body?

17 If the whole body were an eye, where were the hearing? If the whole were hearing, where were the smelling?

18 But now hath God set the members every one of them in the body, as it has *pleased* him.

19 And if they were all one member, where were the body?

20 But now are they many members, yet but one body.

21 And the eye cannot say unto the hand, "I have no need of thee:" nor again the head to the feet, "I have no need of you."

22 Nay, much *more* those members of the body, which seem to be more feeble, are *necessary*:

23 And those members of the body, which we think to be less honourable, upon these we bestow more *abundant* honour; and our uncomely parts have more abundant comeliness.

24 For our comely parts have no need: but God hath *tempered* the body together, having given more abundant honour to that part which *lacked:*

25 That there should be no *schism* in the body; but that the members should have the [*same* care one for another].

26 And whether [one member suffer], *all* the members suffer with it; or [one member be honoured], *all* the members *rejoice* with it.

27 Now *ye* are the [body of Christ], and members in *particular*.

28 And God hath set some in the church, first *apostles*, secondarily *prophets*, thirdly *teachers*, after that *miracles*, then [*gifts of healings*], *helps, governments,* [*diversities* of *tongues*].

29 Are all apostles? are all prophets? are all teachers? are all *workers* of miracles?

30 Have *all* the [gifts of healing]? do *all* speak with tongues? do all interpret?

31 But covet earnestly the *best* gifts: and yet shew I unto you a more excellent way.

When the illustration begins, 12th verse, the mind diverges from the main thought, and those upward and downward turns of voice which we denominate the "wave" instantly telegraph the fact to the listener.

In verse 28 we have the "converse" of massing, these various gifts being pointed out to us by St. Paul as different in themselves, yet requiring the recipients to act in unison, and as helpers one to another.

For our next example we take the 14th chapter of Corinthians for analysis. The student will remember that what is *desirable* is the positive idea; that which is *preferable* as in the example before us; the gift of prophecy is preferred to other spiritual gifts, because of the greater benefit to man which it promises; so that "following after charity," and the desire of "spiritual gifts," are negative goods compared with the positive one of "prophecy." The illustration occurring in the 7th verse requires the "wave"; in the 8th verse the "wave," or "double wave," as it is given on the principal words, indicates the illustration at once, showing that the trumpet and its sounds is not the subject under discussion, but that you make use of it in portraying the value of the gift of "prophecy." The "wave" is executed in about half the time usually, that we employ for the circumflex ⌢ ⌣; its process, however, is the same—viz.: in the upward wave the inflection makes a slight descent and ascent ⌣; in the downward wave ⌢, the directions of tone are reversed—a slight ascent and descent marks its course:

1 Follow after charity, and desire spiritual gifts, but *rather* that ye may *prophesy.*

2 For he that speaketh in an [unknown tongue] speak-

eth not unto *men*, but unto God: for no man understandeth him; howbeit in the spirit he speaketh mysteries.

3 But he that *prophesieth* speaketh unto men to [*edification*, and exhortation, and comfort]

4 He that speaketh in an [unknown tongue] edifieth himself; but he that *prophesieth* edifieth the *church*.

5 I would that ye all spake with tongues, but *rather* that ye *prophesied:* for *greater* is he that prophesieth than he that [speaketh with tongues] (except he interpret), that the church may receive *edifying*.

6 Now, brethren, if I come unto you [speaking with tongues], what shall I profit you, except I shall speak to you either by *revelation*, or by *knowledge*, or by *prophesying*, or by *doctrine?*

7 And even things without *life* giving sound, whether pipe or harp, except they give a *distinction* in the sounds, how shall it be known what is piped or harped?

8 For if the trumpet give an uncertain sound, who shall prepare him to the battle?

9 So likewise *ye*, except ye utter by the tongue words *easy* to be understood, how shall it be *known* what is spoken; for ye shall speak into the air.

10 There are, it may be, so many kinds of voices in the world, and none of them is without signification.

11 Therefore if I know not the *meaning* of the voice, I shall be unto him that speaketh a barbarian, and he that speaketh shall be a barbarian unto *me*.

12 Even so *ye*, forasmuch as ye are [zealous of spiritual

gifts⌋, seek that ye may excel to the ⌈edifying of the church⌋.

13 Wherefore let him that speaketh in an unknown tongue pray that he may interpret.

14 For if I pray in an unknown tongue, my ⌈*spirit* prayeth⌋, but my *understanding* is unfruitful.

15 What is it then? I will pray with the spirit, and I will pray with the *understanding* also : I will *sing* with the spirit, and I will sing with the understanding also.

16 Else when thou shalt bless with the spirit, how shall he that occupieth the ⌈room of the unlearned⌋ say Amen at thy giving of thanks, seeing he understandeth not what thou sayest?

17 For thou verily givest thanks well, but the other is *not* edified.

In the third chapter of James, the subject of the 1st and 2d verses is the perfection which a man has reached who can control his tongue. The illustration of the 3d verse requires the "wave" ⌣ ⌢ to point it as an elucidation of the subject, and not as the subject itself; else, with the upward and downward inflections of voice which belong to the *subject*, the language would be presented to us as that of a horsetamer;— that of the 4th verse as that of a shipbuilder. In the 5th verse the subject is the "tongue," and a "little fire" is the illustration; yet if the "little fire" be discussed with the ╱ ╲ inflections of voice we use in dilating on the "subject," we are as likely to lead our hearers into giving "the fire" the prominent consideration which the subject only should receive :—

1 My brethren, be not many masters, knowing that we shall receive the greater condemnation.

2 For in [many things] we offend *all*. If [any man] offend not in word, the same is a [perfect man], and able also to [*bridle* the whole *body*].

3 Behold, we put bits in the horses' mouths, that they may obey us; and we turn about their whole body.

4 Behold also the ships, which, though they be so great, and are driven of fierce winds, yet are they turned about with a very small helm, whithersoever the governor listeth.

5 Even so [the *tongue*] is a [little member], and boasteth great things. Behold, how [great a matter] a little fire kindleth!

6 And the *tongue* is a fire, a [world of iniquity]; so is the tongue among our members; that it defileth the whole body, and [setteth on *fire*] the course of nature; and it is set on fire of *hell*.

7 For every kind of [beasts, and of birds, and of serpents, and of things in the sea], is tamed, and hath been tamed of *mankind:*

8 But the tongue can no man tame; it is an unruly evil, full of deadly poison.

9 Therewith bless we *God*, even the Father; and therewith curse we *men*, which are made after the *similitude* of God.

10 Out of the same mouth proceedeth [blessing and cursing]. My brethren, these things ought *not* so to be.

11 Doth a fountain send forth at the same place *sweet* water and bitter?

See also Mrs. Browning's poem—" The cry of the children ":

"The young lambs are playing in the meadows," etc.
"But the young, young children, O my brothers!"

the latter being the subject, the first is the illustration.

The following example is from the 18th chapter of Luke:—

1 And he spake a parable unto them to [this *end*], that men ought always to *pray*, and not to faint;

2 Saying, There was in a city a judge, which feared not God, neither regarded *man:*

3 And there was a widow in that city; and she came unto him, saying, "*Avenge* me of mine *adversary.*"

4 And he *would* not for a while: but afterward he said within himself, "Though I fear not God, nor regard man;

5 Yet because this widow troubleth me, I will avenge her, lest by her [continual coming] she *weary* me."

6 And the Lord said, "Hear what the *unjust* judge saith."

7 And shall not *God* avenge his [own elect], which [cry day and night] unto him, though he bear *long* with them?

8 I tell you that he will avenge them *speedily.* Nevertheless when the Son of man cometh, shall he find *faith* [on the earth]?

9 And he spake *this* parable unto certain which trusted in themselves that they were *righteous*, and despised others:

10 Two men went up into the [*temple* to *pray*]; the one a Pharisee and the other a publican.

11 The Pharisee stood and prayed *thus* with himself, "God, I thank thee, that I am not as other men are, extortioners, unjust, adulterers, or even as this publican.

12 I fast twice in the week, I give tithes of all that I *possess*."

13 And the *publican*, standing afar off, would not lift up so much as [his eyes] unto heaven, but *smote* upon his breast, saying, "God be *merciful* to me a sinner."

14 I tell you, this man went down to his house *justified* rather than the other: for every one that [*exalteth* himself] shall be *abased*; and he that *humbleth* himself shall be *exalted*.

15 And they brought unto him also infants, that he would *touch* them: but when his disciples saw it, they rebuked them.

16 But Jesus *called* them unto him, and said, "*Suffer* little children to come unto me, and [*forbid* them not]: for of *such* is the [kingdom of God].

17 Verily I say unto you, "Whosoever shall not receive the [kingdom of God] as a little child shall in no wise enter therein.

18 And a certain ruler asked him, saying, "Good Master, what shall I *do* to inherit eternal life?"

19 And Jesus said unto him, "Why callest thou me good? none is good, save one, that is, God.

20 "Thou knowest the commandments, Do not commit adultery, Do not kill, Do not steal, Do not bear false witness, Honour thy father and thy mother."

21 And he said, "All these have I *kept* from my youth up."

22 Now when Jesus heard these things, he said unto him, Yet lackest thou one thing—sell all that thou hast, and distribute unto the poor, and thou shalt have [treasure in heaven]: and [come, follow me].

1st verse. Psy. positives and negatives.
2d. Illustration, The.
3d. Illustration, "slow quotation" also.
4th. Illustration, and quotation of disparagement.
6th, 7th, 8th. Slow quotation and psychological positives and negatives.
9th. Psy. positives and negatives.
10th. The illustration.
11th, 12th. Psy. pos. and neg., quotation of disparagement.
13th. Psy. positives and negatives, slow quotation.
14th. The teaching.
15th, 16th, 17th. Psy. positives and negatives, and slow quotation.
18th, 19th, 20th, 21st, 22d. Psy. positives and negatives, quotations.

This speech of Bassanio's, from the "casket scene," in the *Merchant of Venice*, affords an excellent example of psychological positives and negatives:

Bass. So may the outward shows be least themselves :
The world is still deceived with ornament.
In *law,* what plea so tainted and corrupt,
But, being seasoned with a gracious voice,
Obscures the [show of evil] ? In *religion,*
What [damned error], but some sober brow,
Will bless it, and approve it with a text,
Hiding the grossness with [fair ornament] ?
There is no vice so simple, but assumes
Some [mark of virtue] on his *outward* parts.
How many cowards, whose hearts are all as false
As [stairs of sand], wear yet upon their chins
The [beards of *Hercules*], and frowning *Mars ;*
Who, inward search'd, have livers white as milk?
And these assume but valour's *excrement,*
To render them redoubted. Look on *beauty,*
And you shall see 'tis purchased by the weight ;
Which therein works a [miracle in nature],
Making them lightest that wear *most* of it :
So are those [crisped snaky golden locks],
Which make such wanton gambols with the wind,
Upon *supposed* fairness, often known
To be the dowry of a second head,
The scull that bred them, in the sepulchre.
Thus ornament is but the [guiled shore]
To a most dangerous sea ; the [beauteous scarf]
Veiling an Indian beauty ; in a word
The *seeming* truth which cunning times put on

To entrap the wisest. Therefore, thou gaudy gold,
(Hard food for Midas,) I will *none* of thee :
Nor none of *thee*, thou pale and common drudge
'Tween man and man : but *thou*, thou meagre *lead*,
Which rather threat'nest, than doth promise aught,
Thy *plainness* moves me more than eloquence,
And *here* choose I : *Joy* be the consequence !

' From lowest place where virtuous things proceed,
The place is dignified by the doer's deed :
Where great additions swell and virtue none,
It is a *dropsied* honour : [good *alone*]
Is good *without* a name, vileness is so : (also vile)
The property by what it is—should go,
Not by the title. She is young, wise, fair,
In these to nature she's immediate heir ;
And these breed *honour:* that is honours scorn,
Which challenges itself as honour born
(And is not *like* the sire). Honours best thrive
When rather from our *acts* we them derive
Than our foregoers : the mere word a slave
Debauched on every tomb ; on every grave
A lying trophy, and (as oft) is dumb
Where dust and damned oblivion is the tomb
Of *honoured* bones indeed."

King Lear. * * * The *usurer* hangs the
cozener.
Through tatter'd clothes small vices do *appear;*

Robes, and furr'd gowns *hide* all. Plate *sin* with gold,
And the strong lance of justice *hurtless* breaks:
Arm it in rags, a pigmy's straw doth *pierce* it.
None does offend, none, I say, none; I'll able 'em:
Take that of me, my friend, who have the power
To seal the accuser's lips. Get thee *glass* eyes;
And, [like a scurvy politician], seem
To see the things thou dost *not.*

§ 3.—ANTAGONISM OF GRAMMATICAL FORMS.

We frequently meet with sentences whose form is antagonistic to their spirit, or meaning. Superficial readers are misled by what *immediately* meets the eye (the *construction* of the sentence) into rendering it with a meaning, spirit, or inflection of voice in accordance with the form. Even careful readers will commit similar errors from the force of long habit, or from false inflections caught from unreflective teachers; the first of these, the result of mannerisms inculcated in early youth; unwittingly, most likely. They do not read that which meets the *understanding*, but that which arrests the *eye* only; else a sentence, interrogative in form but assertive in *meaning*, they would read *assertively*, and not interrogatively, as nine readers out of ten do.

Take an example from Isaiah 40 : 24:

"Have ye not *known?* have ye not *heard?* Hath it not

been *told* you from the *beginning?* have ye not understood from the *foundation* of the earth?"

These clauses are interrogative in form, but decidedly assertive in spirit, as the reader will at once perceive; then shall we follow the *form* in our inflections of voice, or the evident meaning? the "thought," you will say "certainly." In that case the downward or positive inflection is required on the principal words as marked.

Henry VIII—declarative-interrogative:

>*Q. Kath.* Have I lived thus long—(let me speak myself,
>
>Since virtue finds no friends,)—a wife, a true one?
>A woman (I dare say, without vain-glory,)
>Never yet branded with suspicion?
>Have I with all my full affections
>Still met the king? loved him next Heaven? obey'd him?
>Been, out of fondness, superstitious to him?
>Almost forgot my prayers to content him?
>And am I thus rewarded? 'tis not well, lords.
>Bring me a constant woman to her husband;
>One, that ne'er dream'd a joy beyond his pleasure;
>And to that woman, when she has done most,
>Yet will I add, an honour,—a great patience.

As another instance see *Macbeth*, Act 1, Sc. 7:

>*Macb.* "Will it not be received,
>When we have marked with *blood* those sleepy two

Of his own chámber, and used ⌈their very *dággers*⌉,
That *théy* have done 't ? "

Macbeth is not here seeking for information, he is *asserting*.

Look also in the same play for another example—Act 1, Sc. 3:

"Who can be *wíse*, amáted," etc.

In Hebrews 2 : 5 :

"For unto the *ángels* hath he not put in subjection the ⌈world to come⌉, whereof we *spéak ?* "

The next is plainly assertive, although interrogative in form; the upward inflection ╱ should on no account be used at the termination of these clauses. It is not what we do in "*nature*," and those who profess to understand the "art" of reading should scrupulously avoid such an error. James 2 : 4, 5 :

"Are ye not then *pártial* in yourselves, and are become júdges of ⌈evil thóughts⌉ ? "

This thought is viewed from a negative attitude of mind, and requires the negative circumflex, but the cadence or fall of the voice at the termination of the word "thoughts" indicates all that is necessary of the meaning. 5th verse:

"*Héarken*, my belóved brethren, hath not God chosen the ⌈*póor* of this world⌉ rich in *fáith*, and ⌈*héirs* of the kingdom] which he hath promised to them that *love him*?"

The 6th and 7th verses give us examples of the declarative-negative in thought:

6 But ye have *despised* the poor. Do not *rich* men oppress you, and draw you before the [*judgment seats*]?"

7 Do not they blaspheme that [worthy name] by the which ye are *called?*

From Henry VIII—a declarative-negative:

Wol. Most gracious sir,
In humblest manner I require your highness,
That it shall please you to declare, in hearing
Of all these ears, (for where I am robb'd and bound,
There must I be unloosed ; although not there
At once and fully satisfied,) whether ever I
Did broach this business to your highness ; or
Laid any scruple in your way, which might
Induce you to the question on't? or ever
Have to you,—but with thanks to God for such
A royal lady,—spake one the *least* word, might
Be to the prejudice of her present state,
Or touch of her good person? .

In the following instance the spirit is assertive, the form interrogative; the clauses are partly positive in meaning, and partly negative:

6 Is not *this* the fast that I have chosen? To *loose*

the [bônds of wickédness], to *undŏ* the [héavy burdens],
and to let [the oppressed] go *frēe*, and that ye *brēak*
évery yōke?

7 Is it not to [dēal thy *brēad*] to the hūngry, and that
thou *brĭng* [the pŏor] thăt are căst oūt, to thy *hoūse?*
When thou seest the *nāked*, that thou *cŏver* him, and
that thou [hĭde nŏt thȳself] from thĩne own *flĕsh?*—*Isa.*
58 : 6, 7.

From previous explanations the student will readily perceive the reasons for giving certain words in these verses the positive character—certain others the negative; for "massing" certain words conveying but one thought, for using the stronger circumflex instead of the "inflection" on different words.

In *Antony and Cleopatra*, Cleopatra says to Proculeius:

"Know, sir, that I
Will *nŏt* wait pinĭoned at your măster's coūrt,
Nor *ŏnce* be chastised with the sober eye
Of [dŭll Octāvia]. Shall they *hŏist* me up,
And show me to the [shoūting varletry
Of censūring Rōme]? Rather a [*dĭtch* in Egypt]
Be [gentle *grāve*] unto me."

"Rush, in his Division on Interrogative Sentences, says: "The repulsive indignation of this question cannot be fully painted without the fullest measure of interrogative coloring." I maintain that a higher principle determines the inflection of voice in this instance. Strong "negation" is the main thought in

Cleopatra's mind; she is not interrogating Proculeius as to whether she "shall be hoisted up and shown," etc., etc. The sentence is a grammatical interrogative in form, but a decided declarative-negative in meaning—a "psychological negative"—and as these always take the upward inflection ⁄ (or circumflex ⌣, according to the strength of negation), this sentence should be rendered as I have marked it; Cleopatra's meaning being, "They shall *néver* hoist me up," etc.

From *Julius Cæsar*, Act 4, Sc. 2:

Brut. "Judge me, ye gods! wrong I mine enemies?
And if not so, how should I wrong my brother?"

If I do not wrong mine enemies—which might in some sense be excusable—how can it be possible that I should wrong my brother?

Antony over the body of Cæsar:

"He hath brought many *captives* home to Rome,
Whose ransoms did the general coffers *fill*.
Did *this* in Cæsar seem ambitious?
  *   *   *   *   *   *
You all did *see* that on the Lupercal
I thrice presented him a [*kingly crown*],
Which he did thrice *refuse!* was this ambition?"

The student will observe that the downward inflection ⌜ just *above the termination* of a word, indicates not the attitude of mind with regard to the thought the word conveys, but the "falling cadence," which is sometimes natural at the end of a sentence, and merely marks the close, especially in non-interrogatives. In "negative" sentences this falling cadence is preceded by the negative inflection ╱ or circumflex ⌣.

From *Macbeth:*

Witches. Seek to know no more!
Macbeth. I will be satisfied. Deny me this,
And an eternal curse fall on you. Let me know
Why sinks that caldron, and what *noise* is this?

An "imperative" is always understood unless expressed, as in the preceding case, "Let me know."

The following example is a "declarative-negative." The writer means that God never said to an *angel,* "Thou art my son," etc. *Hebrews,* ch. 1:

5 For unto which of the angels said he at any time, "Thou art my Son, this day have I begotten thee?" and again, "I will be to him a Father, and he shall be to me a son."

* * * * * *

13 But to which of the angels said he at any time, "Sit on my right hand until I make thine enemies thy footstool?"

The form of this sentence is antagonistic to its spirit; it is also a "psychological negative."

14 Are they not all [ministering *spirits*], sent forth to *minister* for them who shall be [heirs of *salvation*]?"

INFLECTION. 115

In Romans 4 : 9 :

"Cometh this blessedness then upon the circumcision *only*, or upon the *uncircumcision* also? For we say that *faith* was reckoned to Abraham for *righteousness*."

There are other examples in the same chapter.

2 Corin. 11 : 22:

Are they *Hebrews?* (Interrogative in form, assertive in meaning.) So am *I*. Are they *Israelites?* so am I. Are they the seed of *Abraham?* so am I.

Prov. 24 : 12:

"If thou sayest, 'Behold, we knew it not;' doth not he that pondereth the heart *consider* it? And he that keepeth thy soul doth not he *know* it? and shall not he render every man according to his *works?*"

Matthew 11 : 2, 3:

2 Now when John had heard in the prison the works of Christ, he sent two of his disciples.

3 And said unto him, Art thou he that should come, or do we look for another?

The first part of this latter sentence is plainly assertive—the last is *negative* in spirit, as marked.

There are sentences that are partly interrogative, partly declarative, as this—King Richard III, Gloster to Clarence:

"Brother, good day! what means this armed guard
That *waits* upon your grace?"

These declarative-interrogative sentences are from *Hamlet*, Act 1, Sc. 1. (Enter ghost.)

Bernardo. Looks it not like the *king?*
Mark it, Horatio.   *   *   *   *   *
Horatio. What art thou that usurpest this time of night,
Together with that fair and warlike form,
In which the majesty of buried Denmark
Did sometimes march? by heaven, I charge thee, speak.
Marcellus. 'Tis gone, and will not answer.
Ber. How now, Horatio? You tremble, and look pale :
Is not *this* something *more* than *fantasy?*
Mar. Is it not like the king?

Later in the play where Hamlet is speaking to Polonius—

My lord, you *played* once in the *University* you say?
*   *   *   *
You could for a need study a speech of some dozen or sixteen *lines* which I would set down and *insist* on't?

At the battle-field near Barnet where Warwick is brought wounded, the first words he says abound with this sort of examples. Some of the sentences are in part declarative, in part interrogative.

War. Ah, who is nigh? *come* to me, friend or *foe,*
And tell me, who is *victor,* York or Warwick?

Why ask I that? my [mangled *body*] shews,
[My *blood*, my [want of strength], my sick *heart* shews,]
That I must [*yield* my body] to the *earth*,
And by my fall, the conquest of my foe.
Thus yields the cedar to the *axe's* edge,
Whose arms gave shelter to the [princely *eagle*],
Under whose shade the [ramping *lion*] slept:
Whose [top-branch] overpeer'd *Jove's* spreading tree,
And kept low shrubs from winter's powerful wind.
These *eyes* that now are dimm'd with death's black veil,
Have been [as piercing as the mid-day sun],
To search the [secret treasons] of the world:
The [*wrinkles* in my brow], now fill'd with blood,
Were liken'd oft to [kingly *sepulchres*];
For *who* lived king, but *I* could [dig his *grave*]?
And who durst *smile*, when *Warwick* bent his brow?
Lo, now my glory smear'd in *dust* and blood!
My parks, my walks, my manors that I had,
Even now *forsake* me; and of all my lands,
Is nothing left me but my [*body's* length]!
Why, *what* is *pomp*, rule, reign, but earth and *dust?*
And, live we how we *can*, yet *die* we *must*.

A declarative sentence with an interrogative meaning should be read with the upward intonation.

2. THE CONDITIONAL FORM.

It is antagonistic to the meaning when requiring to be read with the downward inflection, the spirit of the thought being assertive, absolute, not conditional. As an example:—

"If then God does,"

"If it has been proven beyond dispute," etc., etc.

In these verses the spirit of the thought is assertive, the form conditional:—

10 For if, when we were enemies, we were reconciled to God by the [death of his Son], much more, being reconciled, we shall be saved by his life.

* * * * * * *

17 For if by one man's offence death reigned by one; much more they which receive [abundance of grace and of the gift of righteousness] shall reign in *life* by one, Jesus Christ.—*Romans*, chap. 5.

This sentence is in the conditional form, but is assertive in meaning:

"If God be merciful to the sinner, why need he despair?"

The following is an example of conditional form with absolute meaning:—

"If virtue is in itself so lovely, surely then it is its own reward."

The conditional form—assertive in spirit:

"If then God so clothe the grass, which is to-day in the field, and to-morrow is cast into the oven; how much more will he clothe *you*, O ye of little faith."

3. The Imperative Form.

It is antagonistic with the meaning when requiring to be read with the upward inflection, the thought being conditional, contingent, or uncertain.

Othello, Act 3, Sc. 3:

> "Villain, be sure thou prove my love is false:
> Be sure of it; give me the ocular proof;
> * * * * * *
> Or, by the worth of mine eternal soul,
> Thou hadst better have been born a dog
> Than answer my [waked *wrath*].
> * * * * * *
> Make me to see it, or (at the least) so prove it,
> That the probation bear no hinge nor loop
> To hang a doubt on: or woe upon thy life!

Here the thought is "conditional"; Othello does not *desire* that Iago should "prove" his "love" is false; on the contrary, the Moor hopes that the other may not be able to do so; he is positive enough in his meaning in the next line quoted—"Or by the worth," etc. Then we have again the "imperative" in form, but conditional in thought, on the lines: "Make me to see it" (the meaning being, "Unless you can make me to see it"), if you cannot so prove it, that the probation bear no hinge nor loop to hang a doubt on), woe upon thy life";—this last being positive.

The next is imperative in form, but conditional in meaning:—

"Prove to me that person has never done wrong, and I will declare to you that he is worthy of your praise."

This is imperative in form only:

Prove to me, that you know your lessons for to-morrow, and I will believe you.

Example of imperative form with conditional meaning:

Write on both sides of a sheet, and I will throw your manuscript into the fire.

§ 4.—MELODY, AS APPLIED TO THE READING OF POETRY.

John Longmuir, A.M., LL.D., in his "Walker and Webster combined," tells us that Melody, *n.*, is "an agreeable succession of sounds by a single voice, and thus differing from harmony, which consists in the *accordance* of different sounds." Now my experience tells me that most persons who read poetry aloud, do not endeavor to produce an "agreeable succession of sounds"; they attend rather to the symmetrical relation between the duration of "time" and that of "sound," and (mark this, for herein lies the great defect) to the PERIODICAL return of the same effect; they fairly struggle to give us a "harmony," when all that we ask for is a simple, pleasing, *natural* "melody." I emphasize the word "nature," for anything falser to nature than the sing-song manner of rendering poetry that many affect, even public readers, cannot possibly be conceived. That people of known culture should, in the expression of poetry, make more prominent the "rhythm" than the "thoughts" in a poem is simply astonishing. Yet it is matter of experience that many of them make a mere nursery jingle of the noblest and sweetest productions of the poets.

What is poetry? "Poetry is the language of the imagination; poetry is only the highest eloquence of passion; the most vivid form of expression that can be given to our conception of any thing, whether pleasurable or painful, mean or dignified, delightful or distressing. It is the perfect coincidence of the image and the words with the feeling we have, and of which we cannot get rid, in any other way, that gives an instant satisfaction to the thought. This is equally the origin of wit and fancy, of comedy and tragedy, of the sublime and pathetic." Poetry, then, does not consist of rhythmical changes in tone and time, but it is the language which most eloquently and vividly conveys the expression of the passions. Then should the delivery of poetry (as well as prose) be distinguished by the varied tones appropriate to different passions; the "time" in which the successive thoughts are given, depends on our mental valuation of those thoughts, and in my lesson on Time the student will find the necessary principles for guidance in this matter; the emphasis should be controlled by philosophical principles, and we should by no means allow our appreciation of rhythm to betray us into false emphasis, by causing us to give a *corresponding* stress on successive lines without any logical reason for so doing. It remains for me to point out some of the principal errors, into which readers of poetry commonly fall.

1. SIMILARITY OF RHYTHMICAL ACCENT.

This mistake is referred to above; it is a propensity for emphasizing words at a given spot in each successive line; as if, in the first verse of Shelley's "Sensitive Plant," I were deluded by my sense of rhythm into giving it in this manner:

1 A sensitive plant in a *garden* grew,
   And the young winds fed it with *silver* dew,
   And it opened its fan-like *leaves* to the light,
   And closed them beneath the *kisses* of night.

2. SIMILARITY OF ENDING EACH LINE.

This fault in "ending" may be committed by either "stress," or "tone," or a "fall of voice"; the first of these three would be—

"A sensitive plant in a garden *grew*,
   And the young winds fed it with silver *dew*," etc.

The second, by "tone":

   A sensitive plant in a garden grew,
   And the young winds fed it with silver dew, etc.,

the upward inflection (or any other) being systematically given on each concluding word. The "fall of voice" is a peculiar downward cadence given on each concluding word.

3. Similarity by Pause.

This is dividing the lines into equal parts by pausing at stated periods; as if the second verse of the same poem were to be read:

2 And the spring arose—on the garden fair,
  Like the spirit of love—felt everywhere;
  And each flower and herb—on earth's dark breast
  Rose from the dreams—of its wintry rest.

The remainder of this poem may be practised by the pupil, his special care being to avoid the defects against which he is here warned.

For testing whether one has already formed these habits of false rendering, the choice should be given to poems whose measured lines and pronounced rhymes make them peculiarly liable to defective treatment. Of these, familiar to us all, I would suggest the "Bridge of Sighs," the "Psalm of Life," the "May Queen," "Resignation," "John Gilpin," Gray's "Elegy," and Herrick's "To Daffodils," which last I append:

    Fair Daffodils, we weep to see
      You haste away so soon,
    As yet the early rising sun
      Has not attained his noon.
            Stay, stay,

Until the hasting day
               Has run
But to the even-song;
And, having prayed together, we
  Will go with you along.

We have short time to stay as you,
  We have as short a spring;
As quick a growth to meet decay,
  As you, or any thing;
            We die
As your hours do, and dry
            Away,
Like to the summer's rain;
Or as the pearls of morning dew,
Ne'er to be found again.

CHAPTER V.

THE TONES OF THE EMOTIONS.

DIFFERENT emotions and passions are expressed by different intonations of voice. I will not enlarge here upon the lamentable prevalence of false intonations, but we may say that if persons really desirous of cultivating the art of elocution, would but notice the people around them when under the influence of different passions, they would very soon become familiar with the vocal expression natural to the various emotions; they would soon discover that *in nature* we never describe the tender, the affectionate, the beautiful, in semitones; nor deliver sublime passages with abrupt force (which is natural to "rage" and kindred passions). These errors are specified because of their being most common among false intonations. The observant student will find that force, abruptness, time, and pitch are employed in various degrees in giving expression to every emotion that has possession of the mind; he will also perceive that there are some occasions on which soft and tender intonations would be utterly ridiculous; and others again on which force would cause the sentiment to appear disgusting bombast. That state of mind which indicates mere "*thought*," narratives or descriptions, which represent things as they are in themselves, without reference to our relationship to them, require an intonation which is unemotional; that which we call the *didactic,* or simply intellectual. Force of voice is employed in the expression of rage, wrath, danger, horror; and force combined with the aspirate gives us astonishment, exultation, or surprise—according to the degrees of aspiration and force used. Abrupt force gives us a greater degree of rage, wrath, anger, or impatience; then with less force, much less, and equal abruptness, we have mirth and raillery. All sentiments that embrace the idea of deliberation we give in lengthened intonations, as sorrow, grief, respect, veneration, dignity, apathy, contrition. I speak of this here, as these passions in their expression are opposed to those more violent emotions, which will not bear repression, but take instant relief in "abrupt force." The quality of voice in anger and in imperative authority is "loud"; in grief, modesty, commiseration, "soft"; secresy is "whispered"; hate is "aspirated." We hear the "head voice" in the whine of peevishness; in the querulous, in the high tremulous pitch of mirth, in the piercing scream of terror; we hear the *head voice* in all of these, but they are distinguished from each other by the different degrees of force, of time, and of emphasis or stress, that are also employed in conjunction with it.

A softened modulation of voice is required by humility, modesty, shame, doubt, irresolution, apathy, fatigue, caution, tranquillity—these on *whole tones* generally, and with different degrees of time and

THE TONES OF THE EMOTIONS. 127

stress; the same degree of gravity in combination with the semitone gives us sorrow, pity, grief.

Take, for example, a few lines that are capable of being given with different meanings, according to the intonation employed. These spoken by Constance in King John will serve the purpose:

> *Const.* Gone to be married! gone to swear a peace!
> False blood to false blood join'd! gone to be friends!
> Shall Lewis have Blanch? and Blanch those provinces?
> It is not so.

Deliver this passage on varied semitones, with the *vowels* all pronounced in *slow* time, and you have "sorrow." The relative acuteness or gravity of the semitones used on this passage is indicated by the following arrangement:

```
                            6 and Blanch those provinces!
                          5 Shall Lewis have Blanch?
                       4 gone to be friends!
              2 gone to swear a peace!
  1 Gone to be married!
                 3 False blood to false blood join'd!    7 It is not so!
```

Now pronounce the lines on whole tones but with the voice skipping about up and down the scale *ad libitum*, but not with regularity, neither reaching a very high nor a very low key; literally tripping about among the notes within a reasonable compass, like this for instance:

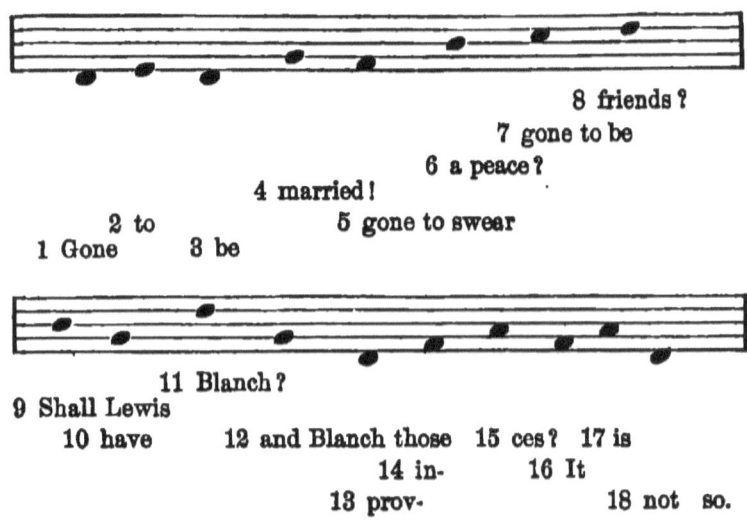

The vowel sounds are all pronounced in quick time; they are not dwelt upon as in sorrow, but are sounded, and instantly the voice skips to another word—now we have the intonation of joy.

To render the passage with "*anger*" "abrupt force" is used, the vowel sounds are "exploded" rather than spoken, the chest voice is to be employed here, and with great force; the voice does not rise to so high a key as in joy, nor fall to so low a key as in sorrow; yet avoid the "monotone," which is the symbol of a very different passion.

Now give the lines with surprise; in portraying this emotion the voice will travel through several whole tones on almost every word; the time is slow in unmixed surprise, but the leading feature of surprise is the "partial aspirate"; the words being partly spoken, partly *breathed* forth.

This little example may be given with sarcasm,

with scorn, hate, affirmation, exclamation, interrogation, as desired. For the analysis of these tones the pupil is referred to the division dealing with each.

§ 1.—THE OROTUND VOICE.

This is the symbol of sublimity. Longinus says, that "the mind is elevated by it (sublimity) and so sensibly affected as to *swell* in *transport* and inward pride as if what is only heard or read, were its own invention." Now this is exactly the action of the voice in expressing a sense of sublimity; it *swells*—that is, it *increases* in volume, roundness, power, at each impulse; there is no explosiveness, but a gradual increase of force on each word; and we will borrow the character used in music to describe a similar effect, as the sign of the "orotund"—namely, the "crescendo" <.

The grand, the magnificent, etc., creating kindred emotions in the mind, call also for the "orotund," in giving that feeling expression; and in describing these emotions, a greater or lesser degree of the orotund is required according to the force of motive power. In practising the exercises illustrative of this principle of intonation, the pupil will use the base voice, and on the principal words in the passage give the orotund as marked; each word begins with a certain degree of force, but that force is slowly increased, and pauses in its volume (but does not decrease) after each impulse. A close acquaintance with the meanings, and shades of meaning, in words sometimes used synonymously, will be the best director in deciding the degrees of the orotund required in different cases; that which is "great" requires a lesser degree than that which is grand; that which is simply "grand," less than the "sublime," etc. I quote briefly from *Crabbe's Synonymes* as an assistance to younger pupils in discriminating the "tones" requisite: "Great simply designates extent; *grand* includes likewise the idea of excellence and superiority. A *great* undertaking characterizes only the extent of the undertaking; a *grand* undertaking bespeaks its superior excellence. Grand and sublime are both superior to great; but the former marks the dimension of greatness, the latter, from the Latin *sublimis*, designates that of height. A scene may be either grand or sublime: it is grand, as it fills the imagination with its immensity; it is sublime, as it elevates the imagination beyond the surrounding and less important objects. There is something grand in the sight of a vast army moving forward as it were by one impulse; there is something peculiarly sublime in the sight of huge mountains and craggy cliffs of ice shaped into various fantastic forms. Grand may be said either of the works of art or nature. The Egyptian pyramids or the ocean are both grand objects; a tempestuous ocean is a sublime object. 'Grand' is sometimes applied to the mind; sublime is applied both to the thoughts and the expressions. There is a '*grandeur*' of conception in the writings of Milton; there is a '*sublimity*' in the inspired writings, which far surpass all human productions."

As an example of the orotund see these lines from *Julius Cæsar*, Act 1, Sc. 3:

He doth bestride the narrow world
Like a Colossus ; and we petty men
Walk under his huge legs.

Here is one of many instances from "*Antony and Cleopatra*":

  Cleo. I dream'd, there was an emperor Antony;—
O, such another sleep, that I might see
But such another man !
  Dol. If it might please you,
  Cleo. His face was as the heavens; and therein stuck
A sun, and moon; which kept their course, and lighted
The little O, the earth.
  Dol. Most sovereign creature,
  Cleo. His legs bestrid the ocean: his rear'd arm
Crested the world: his voice was propertied
As all the tuned spheres, and that to friends;
But when he meant to quail and shake the orb,
He was as rattling thunder.
                                          —*Act 5, Sc. 3.*

The psychological positives and negatives are not incompatible with this or any other intonation: the inflections, indicating the positive and negative frames of mind, merely carry the required intonation in an upward or downward direction, according to necessity.

The following is from *King Lear, Act 4, Sc.* 5 :

  Edg. Come on, sir; here's the place:—stand still.—
      How fearful
And dizzy 'tis, to cast one eyes so low !

The crows and choughs, that wing the midway air,
Shew scarce so gross—as beetles; half way down *mod.**
Hangs one that gathers samphire,—dreadful trade!
Methinks, he seems no bigger—than his head: *mod.*
The fishermen, that walk upon the beach,
Appear—like mice; and yon' tall anchoring bark, *mod.*
Diminish'd to her cock; her cock, a—buoy, *mod.*
Almost too small for sight: The murmuring surge,
That on the unnumber'd idle pebbles chafes,
Cannot be heard so high:—I'll look no more; *mod.*
Lest my brain turn, and the deficient sight
Topple down headlong.

The greater objects naturally take the orotund, the lesser a modulated tone, akin to their littleness; the great height is admirably delineated by the similitudes employed; the distances are pictured by the swell of the voice on each "subject," and its sudden fall to a much modified key on the comparisons.

Hamlet, Act 3, Sc. 1:—

"Majesty
Dies not *alone*, but—like a gulf doth draw
What's near it with it. It's a massy wheel
Fixed on the summit of the highest mount;
To whose huge spokes ten thousand—lesser things *mod.*
Are mortised and adjoined; which, when it falls,

---

* Moderate the tone.

moderate the tone.
Each—small annexment, petty consequence,
Attends the boist'rous ruin."

In practising this exercise, be careful to increase the volume of tone on the words marked with the "crescendo" <.

The following example is from Henry Kirke White:

"Yea, He doth come,—the mighty champion comes,
Whose potent spear shall give thee thy death wound,
Shall crush the conqueror of conquerors,
And desolate stern desolation's lord;
Lo where He cometh! the Messiah comes!
The King! the Comforter! the Christ! He comes
To burst the bonds of death and overturn
The [power of time]."

In the following exercise the pupil will perceive an example of the "parenthesis," and also of the intonation employed in describing the beautiful—the diminuendo:—

"It is not only in the sacred fane
That homage should be paid to the most High.
There is a temple,—one not made with hands—
The vaulted firmament; far in the woods,
Almost beyond the sound of city chime,
At intervals heard through the breezeless air;
When not the limberest leaf is seen to move
(Save where the linnet lights upon the spray),

When not a flow'ret bends its little stalk
(Save where the bee alights upon the bloom),
There, rapt in gratitude, in joy, and love,
The man of God will pass the Sabbath noon;
Silence his praise, his disembodied thoughts
Loosed from the [load of words], will high ascend
Beyond the empyrean."

—*The Worship of God in the Solitude of the Woods.*—JAMES GRAHAME, 1765–1811.

This passage from Othello gives us an excellent exercise on the "orotund":—

"Like to the Pontic sea,
Whose icy current and compulsive course
Ne'er feels retiring ebb—but keeps due on
To the Propontic and the Hellespont,
Even so my murderous* thoughts with violent pace
Shall ne'er look back, ne'er ebb to humble love,
Till that a capable and wide revenge
Swallow them up."

—*Othello, Act 3, Sc. 3.*

§ 2.—ABRUPT FORCE.

This is the sign of anger, wrath, danger, etc. Public speakers of all sorts, clergymen, actors, orators, etc., almost all suffer sooner or later, when ignorant of the

---

* This word is substituted for "bloody," which is the true reading.

correct mode of using "abrupt force." They strain their voices to such an extent in passionate utterance, that very soon the voice "breaks," or inflammatory and other affections of the bronchiæ are induced which soon incapacitate the unfortunates for public speaking of any kind. Their mistake is in endeavoring to give abrupt force with the throat and head voices, instead of the *chest* voice, which should be used the same as in the orotund. For the cultivation of this particular intonation, instead of the "swell" of the "orotund," the word is "exploded" with equal force at one impulse; the vowels are all short, given instantaneously, and each consonant rendered with intensity—if I may so express it.

If in the exercise which follows the pupil *wills* that his voice come from the lowest part of the chest, and that each word be expelled with one sudden heaving of the diaphragm, he will find that he has at his command a quality of voice for expressing passion, which he may use *ad libitum* and for almost any length of time, without feeling fatigue, and with no danger of tearing "passion to tatters to very rags—to split the ears of the groundlings."

The queen says:—

"By heaven! I will acquaint his majesty
Of those gross taunts I often have received!"

Exercise:—(Vowels all abrupt like this: "What? threat you me," etc.)

> *Gloster.* What? threat you me with telling of the king?

Tell him, and spare not: look, what I have said
I will avouch, in *presence* of the king:
Ere you were queen, aye, or your husband king,
I was a pack horse in his great affairs.
A weeder-out of his proud adversaries,
A liberal rewarder of his friends;
In all which time, you and your husband
Grey, were factious for the house of Lancaster
And Rivers! so were you!
A flourish, trumpets; strike alarum, drums!
 * * * * Strike, I say!"
      —*Richard III.*, Act 1, Sc. 3.

Exercise:

"Ruin seize thee, ruthless king!
Confusion on thy banners wait;
Though fanned by conquest's crimson wing,
They mock the air with idle state.
Helm nor hauberk's twisted mail,
Nor e'en thy virtues, tyrant, shall avail
To save thy secret soul from nightly fears,
From Cambria's curse, from Cambria's tears!"
      —*The Bard.*—THOMAS GRAY.

The following is an exercise for the practice of abrupt force; but it is of equal importance in the exercise it gives us for the recovery of the voice on a low key, after reaching a climax on a high key. The first sentence as far as "fiend" is pronounced on a low key with mere force (not abrupt); then on a higher key, with abrupt force, as far as "anything"; then recover the voice on a low key at "that's due," rising higher

THE TONES OF THE EMOTIONS. 137

and higher until "come" has been pronounced. Now recover the *low* key at "O," rise higher and higher, recover the *low* key at "some" (giving the next two words on the same key), raise the voice slightly at "thou," reaching gradually the highest point of the "chest voice"; after the word "amend" recover the low key; raise it again at "I am," etc.; recover low key at "villain-like"; raise the key somewhat on "lesser," thence descend gradually to a very low tone, at which finish.

Post. Ay, so thou dost,
       (*Coming forward.*)
Italian fiend!—Ah me, most credulous fool,
Egregious murderer, thief, any thing
That's due to all the villain's past, in being.
To come!—O, give me cord, or knife, or poison,
Some upright justicer! Thou, king, send out
For torturers ingenious; it is I
That all the abhorred things of the earth amend,
By being worse than they. I am Posthumus,
That kill'd thy daughter:—villain-like, I lie;
That caused a lesser villain than myself,
A sacrilegious thief, to do't.

§ 3.—CLIMAX.

This means "ascent"; it is a figure in rhetoric in which a sentence rises as it were step by step; or a *series* of sentences or particulars rise in importance or dignity to the close, and the *voice* must correspond with this upward progress and increased power by rising in "pitch" and in "force." "Cæsura," as applied here, means "the pause" which we make in reading, in order to call attention to, and to give weight to the clause immediately following.

I append several examples for the practice of "climax." After a climax has been reached on any sentence or series of sentences, the voice *resumes* on a very much lower key.

"A hungry, lean-faced villain,
A mere anatomy, a mountebank,
A thread-bare juggler and a "fortune-teller":
A needy, hollow-eyed, sharp-looking wretch,
          climax.
A [living dead-man]:—this pernicious slave
Forsooth took on him [as a conjuror],
And gazing in mine eyes, feeling my pulse,
And with no face, as 'twere outfacing me,
Cries out—(*cæsura*)—I was possessed!"

"And *I*, forsooth, in *love!* I, that have been love's whip,
A critic; nay, a night-watch constable;
      climax.
A domineering pedant—o'er the boy,
Than whom no mortal so magnificent!
This wimpled,* whining, purblind, wayward boy;
This [senior-junior], [giant-dwarf]—Dan Cupid,
Regent of love-rhymes, lord of folded arms,
The anointed sovereign of sighs and groans,
Liege of all loiterers and malcontents,
Dread prince of plackets,† king of codpieces,

---

* Hooded.   † Petticoats.

Sole imperator and great general
Of trotting paritors.—O my little heart—(*cæsura*) [*climax* above "paritors"]
And I to be a corporal of his field,
And wear his colors like a tumbler's hoop.
What I! I love! I sue! I seek a wife! [*climax* above "wife"]
A woman that is [like a German clock],—(*sim. disap.*)
Still a repairing; ever out of frame,
And never going right, being a watch,—(*cæsura*)
But being watch'd that it may still go right."

The word "climax" is introduced in the proper places in these exercises, also the "cæsura"; the first, *after* the series, or when the climax has been reached; the second, *before* the sentence to which you wish to lend "weight." "Cadence" is that fall of the voice which indicates the approaching end of a sentence or passage.

"Sink or swim, live or die, survive or perish,—I give my hand and my heart to this vote.
(*Raise the pitch.*) Read this declaration at the head of the army, and every sword shall be drawn from its scabbard and the solemn vow uttered to maintain it—(*cæsura*) —or to perish on the bed of honor. Let them hear it, who heard the first roar of the enemies' cannon. Let them see it, who saw their brothers and their sons fall on the field of Bunker-hill and in the streets of Lexington and Concord,—(*cæsura*)—and the very walls shall cry out for its support.

I leave off as I began, that, live-or die, survive or perish, —(*cæsura*)—I am for the declaration."

§ 4.—FORCE.

The practice of simple force adds to the voice dignity and volume. This admirable roundness of tone is opposed to the disagreeable squeak and repulsive nasal twang characteristic of many. Force differs from "abrupt force" merely in its slow, deliberate utterance, when compared with "the explosiveness" of the latter.

Give with the bass voice the following exercise, *increasing* the force at the points indicated by *ff*, *fff*, *ffff* :—

Macbeth, Act 3, Sc. 5:

f What man dare, I dare:
Approach thou like the rugged Russian bear,
The arm'd rhinoceros or the hyrcan tiger;
Take any shape but that, and my firm nerves
Shall never tremble. *ff* Or, be alive again,
And dare me to the desert with thy sword;
If trembling I inhibit thee, protest me
The baby of a girl. *fff* Hence, horrible shadow!
ffff Unreal mockery, hence!

§ 5.—THE DIMINUENDO.

The diminuendo ➤ is the symbol of affection, tenderness, beauty, and love. This tone is commenced with a certain degree of volume at each impulse, but gradually vanishes away to inaudibility. The fault with most readers and reciters is that they have no knowledge of the operation of nature on the human voice, when it gives utterance to thoughts of "love," or to descriptions of the "beautiful." These superficial students select the semitone (usually), as being the nearest approach to the tone of which they are in quest, and the consequence is that some of the sweetest and tenderest passages in the language, the most vivid descriptions of the beautiful, the impassioned eloquence of love—all are given with a lugubrious intonation, absurd in the extreme. The semitone is the symbol of sorrow, as has been observed before; and in portraying grief and the like, the minor keys, peculiarly characteristic of the "plaintive," are employed. Listen to your friend's raptures on a lovely starlight or moonlight night; to his description of a charming landscape which he has just enjoyed; if you *could* be the third party to a love-scene! note how each impulse of the voice is commenced with a fullness of voice, a roundness of intonation, which *gradually* dies away, but at no period of the impulse merges into a half tone.

By an "impulse" I desire to indicate the amount of intonation employed on one word generally—one effort of the voice; and the vanishing movement is made on a *whole tone* not on a half tone; a term which happily expresses this intonation is the "imperceptible vanish." The pupil must exercise taste and judgment in the use of this tone, giving it on the principal words only in the sentence, and the degree of power must be determined by the depth or the earnestness of the words.

Here follow some exercises on the *diminuendo* >.
Ingoldsby:

> O sw>eet and beaut>iful is night
> When the silver m>oon is high,
> And countless st>ars, like clustering gems,
> Hang spar>kling in the sky ;
> While the b>almy br>eath of the sum>mer breeze
> Comes whis>pering down the glen,
> And o>ne f>ond v>oice al>one is heard,
> O Night is lo>vely then.

Twelfth Night, Act 1, Sc. 1

> If music be the food of love, play on,
> Give me exc>ess of it ; that surfeiting,
> The appetite may sicken and so die—
> That str>ain ag>ain ;—it had a dy>ing f>all :
> O it came o'er my ear like the sw>eet so>uth,
> That breathes upon a b>ank of vi>olets,
> Stealing and g>iving o>dor.

The contemplation of the "beautiful," whether sensibly or mentally, tends to fill the beholder with pleasure; and this delight is shown in the countenance, so that a smiling or pleased expression of face (which it is so easy to assume) will materially aid the reader in giving the vocal expression.

The diminuendo requires moderate force at the beginning of each word, which you desire to mark by it; that moderate force should *gradually* become less and less, until at the termination of the word it has vanished into inaudibility, or has become a mere point of sound. Perhaps this little illustration will convey a better idea of my meaning to some minds: OOOoooo. Pronounce the word "oh" with lessening degrees of force; prolonging the word, but not repeating it on each impulse; then practise the intonation on a higher key, using the same word, "oh," "OOOoooo"; now practise it on a lower; then change freely about from one key to another.

The next exercise is a very easy example of the vanishing movement, and pupils who find any difficulty in acquiring it, would do well to practise with this before taking the two that have been already given:

"In such an hour are told the hermit's beads;
　With the white sail the seaman's hymn floats by:
Peace be with all! whate'er their varying creeds,
　With all that send up holy thoughts on high!
Come to me, my boy—by Guadalquiver's vines,
By every stream of Spain, as day declines,
　Man's prayers are *mingled* in the sky."
　　　　　　　　　　　　　—*Mrs. Hemans.*

"Lament of Mary Queen of Scots, at the approach of Spring":

　"My son, my son, may kinder stars
　　Upon thy fortune shine;
　And may those pleasures gild thy reign,

That ne'er wad blink on mine.
God keep thee frae thy mother's faes;
  Or turn their hearts to thee:
And where thou meetst thy [mother's friend],
  Remember him for me."
            —*Burns.*

A beautiful bit of word-painting from "Sella's Fairy Slippers":

"My friend
Named the strange growths, the pretty coralline;
The dulse with crimson leaves, and streaming far,
Sea-thong and sea-lace. Here the tangle spread
Its broad thick fronds, with pleasant bowers beneath;
And oft we trod a waste of pearly sands
Spotted with rosy shells, and thence looked in
At caverns of the sea whose rock-roofed halls
Lay in blue twilight."
            —*William Cullen Bryant.*

In the following the degree of pleasurable thought increases at each verse—so should the diminuendo be more and more marked:—

There are some hearts [like wells green-mossed and deep]
    As ever summer saw;
And cool their water is—yea, cool and sweet;—
    But you must come to draw.
They hoard not, yet they rest in calm content,
    And not unsought will give;
They can be quiet with their wealth unspent,
    So self-contained they live.

And there are some [like springs that bubbling burst],
    To follow dusty ways,
And run with offered cup to quench his thirst
    Where the tired traveler strays;
That never ask the meadows if they want
    What is their joy to give;
Unasked their lives to other life they grant,
    So self-bestowed they live!

And One is—[like the ocean, deep and wide];
    Wherein all waters fall
That girdles the broad earth, and draws the tide,
    Feeding and bearing all.
That broods the mists, and sends the clouds abroad,
    That takes again to give;
Even the great and loving heart of God,
    Whereby all Love doth live.
        —*Living Waters*, by *Caroline Spencer*.

In this example from "Byron" the "imperceptible vanish" should be employed on almost every word to depict the sweetness:

    *   *   * 'Tis sweet to hear,
At midnight on the blue and moonlit deep,
The song and oar of Adria's gondolier,
By distance mellowed, o'er the waters sweep;
'Tis sweet to see the evening stars appear;
'Tis sweet to listen, as the night-winds creep
From leaf to leaf; 'tis sweet to view on high
The rain-bow, based on ocean, span the sky.

* * 'Tis sweet to be awakened by the lark,
Or lulled by falling waters; sweet the hum
Of bees, the [voice of girls], the [song of birds],
The [lisp of children], and their earliest words.

In these lines no touch of the "semitone" must be given, but strictly the "diminuendo," to give a correct interpretation of the sentiment, in which "sorrow" takes no part:

"How beautiful is night!
A dewy freshness fills the silent air,
No mist obscures, nor cloud, nor speck, nor stain,
Breaks the serene of Heaven:
In full-orb'd glory yonder moon divine
Rolls through the dark blue depths.
Beneath her steady ray
The desert circle spreads
Like the round ocean, girdled with the sky."

§ 6.—THE SEMITONE.

This is the symbol of sorrow and grief, but from these spring other emotions, which are expressed by the semitone in a greater or a lesser degree, according to their intensity or the contrary; some of these are penitence, condolence, compassion, mercy, commiseration, pity. When *sorrow* for evils endured, or expected, are at the foundation of fatigue, pain, or supplication, then are these emotions depicted by the semitone. In "sorrow" the "time" is slow; and this "slow time" is naturally secured by *dwelling* on the vowel sounds in the words, and not by "*pauses*" between the words. Then the "key" should be now high, now low, as taste and judgment direct. Some persons succeed in giving the semitone, but they do not portray "sorrow" when they speak in a single, monotonous whine. Vary the semitone, let it be now grave, now acute, and so on. If the pupil's ear is not sufficiently familiar with the difference between tones and "half tones," they should be sounded on the piano, and the class made to accompany with their voices. They should ascend and descend on whole tones, then on half tones, and eventually they should be required to pronounce with the pianist a "broken" melody—tones and half tones being given at irregular distances. Practice first with this intonation the passage from *King John*, given in the first part of this division; then take the following as an exercise. The second line requires a higher key than the first line, and the third line a *lower* key than either; the fourth line may perhaps be given at about the same altitude as the first. For the second verse vary the arrangement of keys as you please, being careful to keep within the bounds of good taste.

Few and short were the prayers we said,
And we spoke not a word of sorrow;
But we steadfastly gazed on the face that was dead,
And we bitterly thought of the morrow.

We thought as we hollowed his narrow bed,
And smoothed down his lonely pillow,

> That the foe and the stranger would tread o'er his head,
> And we far away on the billow.
> —*Burial of Sir John More, by Rev. Chas. Wolfe.*

A sad reflection, from the "Nevermore," by Dante Gabriel Rossetti:

> "Look in my face; my name is [Might-have-been];
> I am also called—"No-more," "Too-late," "Farewell";
> Unto thine ear, I hold the dead sea-shell
> Cast up, thy life's foam-fretted feet between;
> Unto thine eyes, the glass where that is seen
> Which had Life's form, and Love's, but by my spell,
> Is now a shaken shadow intolerable,
> Of ultimate things unuttered, the frail screen."

These two verses, from Mrs. Browning's "Bertha in the Lane," require a plaintive minor key, with a slight occasional touch of the diminuendo:

> "And, dear Bertha, let me keep
>   On my hand this little ring,
> Which at nights, when others sleep,
>   I can still see glittering;
> Let me wear it out of sight,
> In the grave,—where it will light
> All the dark up, day and night.
>
> "On that grave drop not a tear!
>   Else, though fathom-deep the place,
> Through the woollen shroud I wear
>   I shall feel it on my face.

Rather smile there, blessed one ;
Thinking of me in the sun,—
Or forget me, smiling on !"

This pathetic morceau, from Robert Buchanan's "Little Ned," requires semitones, but not a great variety of them; the range should be limited as in repressed grief:

* * . "And one cold day in winter time, when mother
Had gone away into the snow, and we
Sat close for warmth and cuddled one another ;
He put his little head upon my knee,
And went to sleep, and would not stir a limb,
But looked quite strange and old ;
And when I shook him, kissed him, spoke to him,
He smiled ;—and grew so cold.
Then I was frightened and cried out, and none
Could hear me ; while I sat and nursed his head
Watching the whitened window, while the sun
Peeped in upon his face and made it red,
And I began to sob,—till mother came,
Knelt down, and screamed, and named the good God's name,
And told me he was dead.
And when she put his night-gown on, and weeping
Placed him among the rags upon his bed,
I thought that brother Ned was only sleeping,
And took his little hand and felt no fear.
But when the place grew gray and cold and drear,
And the round moon over the roofs came creeping,
And put a silver shade

All round the chilly bed where he was laid,
I cried, and was afraid."

Here are two verses from the poem which relates "Little Gretchen's" wanderings on "New Year's eve":—

* * * * * *

"And she remembered her of tales her mother used to tell,
And of the cradle-songs she sang, when summer's twilight fell;
Of good men, and of angels, and of the Holy Child,
Who was cradled in a manger, when winter was most wild;
Who was poor, and cold, and hungry, and desolate, and lone;
And she *thought* the song had told, he was ever with his own;
And all the poor and hungry, and forsaken ones are his,—
'How good of him to look on me in such a place as this!'

* * * * * *

In her scant and tattered garments, with her back against the wall,
She sitteth cold and rigid; she answers to no call.
They have lifted her up fearfully, they shuddered as they said,
'It was a bitter, bitter night! the child is frozen dead.'
The angels sang their greeting for one more redeemed from sin;
Men said, 'It was a bitter night: would no one let her in?'

And they shivered as they spoke of her, and sighed.
  They could not see
How much of *happiness* there was after that misery."

§ 7.—JOY.

The joyous intonation is characterized by a light, quick "skipping" of the voice, up and down the scale; not reaching a very high nor a very low key, unless the emotion is excessive; the greater the degree of joy, the greater the range of voice, and the faster the time in changing from one key to another. The words are pronounced on whole tones, but the voice skips about up and down the scale, but not with regularity—tripping about among the notes within a reasonable compass. The vowel sounds are all pronounced in quick time; they are not dwelt upon as in sorrow. If a mere "pleasure" is taken in the thoughts expressed, the intonation is the same, but the range of notes is contracted, and the "time" slower than in excessive joy. In the following exercise we have simply pleasure in the thoughts conveyed; occasionally the diminuendo is required:—

"On her white breast, a sparkling cross she wore,
Which Jews might kiss, and infidels adore.
Her lively looks a sprightly mind disclose,
Quick as her eyes, and as unfix'd as those:
Favors to none, to all she smiles extends;
Oft she rejects, but never once offends.
Bright as the sun, her eyes the gazers strike,
And like the sun, they shine on all alike.

> Yet graceful ease, and sweetness void of pride,
> Might hide her faults, if belles had faults to hide;
> If to her share some female errors fall,
> Look on her face and you'll forget them all.
> —*Rape of the Lock.*

The next is of the same order, but the "diminuendo" is more prominent than in the preceding example:

> "O the pleasing, pleasing anguish,
> When we love, and when we languish!
>   Wishes rising,
>   Thoughts surprising,
>   Pleasure courting,
>   Charms transporting,
>   Fancy viewing,
>   Joys ensuing,
> O the pleasing, pleasing anguish."
> —*Rosamond,* Act 1, Sc. 2.

A verse or two from S. H. Dana's "Pleasure-boat" will give good practice for the joyous intonation.

> Come, hoist the sail, the furl let go!
>   They're seated side by side;
> Wave chases wave in pleasant flow;
>   The bay is fair and wide.
>
> The ripples lightly tap the boat,
>   Loose! Give her to the wind!
> She shoots ahead; they're all afloat;
>   The strand is far behind.
>   *   *   *   *

Careening to the wind, they reach,
  With laugh and call, the shore.
They've left their footprints on the beach,
  But them, I hear no more.

§ 8.—THE ASPIRATE.

This is the symbol of hate, secrecy, surprise, with different modifications of *tone* for each; that is, the aspirate is the special characteristic of each, but it alone would by no means constitute the expression of the emotion. Hate is expressed usually on one of the *lowest* keys given with force, and employs also the guttural vibration; these, with a strong degree of the aspirate, depicts the passion. Secrecy takes more of the aspirate, and less vocal force, and is delivered on a higher key than hate. Surprise takes much less of the aspirate than the preceding; it is given on a higher key also: if the emotion is pleasurable, the voice travels in an upward direction through several keys at each impulse; if the surprise be disagreeable, the voice travels on a downward direction through several keys at each impulse.

Earnestness, intensity, horror, and curiosity are all marked by the aspirate. The pupil on reflection will perceive that the passions spoken of first, "hate," etc., or their primal causes, are in one way or another at the foundation of earnestness, intensity, and so on; that they are all akin—branches of the same family; for hate is the foundation of horror; a desire, or expectation of surprise, is at the root of curiosity. Self-love, in some form or other, is the basis both of hate and of earnestness; and in intensity the feeling that produces the *intense* expression is so important to us, that nature feels that common vocal utterance is inadequate to express the feeling (and here self-love may be at work again), so she endeavors to add strength to her enunciation by the aspirate.

As an exercise for the practice of the aspirate in hate, take the following from the *Merchant of Venice*, Act 3, Sc. 1:—

Shy. To bait fish withal: if it will feed nothing else, it will feed my revenge. He hath disgraced me, and hindered me of half a million; laughed at my losses, mocked at my gains, scorned my nation, thwarted my bargains, cooled my friends, heated mine enemies; and what's his reason? I am a Jew. Hath not a Jèw eyes? hath not a Jew hands, organs, dimensions, senses, affections, passions? fed with the same food, hurt with the same weapons, subject to the same diseases, healed by the same means, warmed and cooled by the same winter and summer, as a Christian is? if you prick us, do we not bleed? if you tickle us, do we not laugh? if you poison us, do we not die? and if you wrong us, shall we not revenge? if we are like you in the rest, we will resemble you in that. If a Jew wrong a Christian, what is his humility? revenge; if a Christian wrong a Jew, what should his sufferance be by Christian example? why, revenge. The villainy you teach me, I will execute; and it shall go hard, but I will better the instruction.

The prevailing passion in this speech is *hate;* the

interrogatives are so in form merely; they are assertive in spirit; there are points at which a climax is reached—the mode and the circumstances requiring it are explained under the section "Climax." Contempt, scorn, and the sneer, all take more or less of the aspirate; but it is not their chief characteristic.

In the next example the words underlined with a running mark 〰〰 require the aspirate; and as an *exercise* I would advise the aspirate to be given very strongly; not but that it might be correct to read the lines with less of the "aspirate," but it is the *culture* of that particular quality of tone that we want, and skilful surgeons usually cut beyond the wound to make the cure complete:—

Enter Marcius.

Com. Who's yonder,
That does appear as he were flay'd? O gods!
He has the stamp of Marcius; and I have
Before-time seen him thus.

Mar. Come I too late?

Com. The shepherd knows not *thunder* from a tabor
More than I know the sound of Marcius' tongue
From every meaner man's.

Mar. Come I too late?

Com. Ay, if you come not in the blood of others,
But mantled in your own.
—*Coriolanus*, Act 1, Sc. 6.

This from *King John* is a fine exercise:—

"If thou didst but consent
To this most cruel act do but despair,
And if thou wantst a cord, the smallest thread
Will serve to strangle thee, a rush will be a beam,
To hang thee on ; or wouldst thou drown thyself,
(Fast time.)
Put but a little water in a spoon,
And it shall be as all the ocean,
Enough to stifle such a villain up !
I do suspect thee very grievously,

Aspirate intensity:

> But see how swift advance and shift
> Trees behind trees—row by row.
> How cleft by cleft, rocks bend and lift
> Their frowning foreheads as we go !
> The giant snouted crags—ho ! ho !
> How they snort, and how they blow.
> *—Faust.*

§ 9.—PRAISE.

Let us mark the differences between the intonations of "joy" and of "praise." In joy the voice skips about from one tone to another;—the movement is discrete. In "praise" the voice moves steadily and concretely through several tones at each impulse, and the word is finished on a higher key (several keys rather) than the one on which it was commenced. These kind of "notes" will give an idea of the intonation of joy:

ing-kindness: according unto the multitude of thy tender mercies blot out my transgressions.

2 Wash me thoroughly from mine iniquity, and cleanse me from my sin.

3 For I acknowledge my transgressions: and my sin is ever before me.

4 Against thee, thee only, have I sinned, and done this evil in thy sight: that thou mightest be justified when thou speakest, and be clear when thou judgest.

5 Behold, I was shapen in iniquity; and in sin did my mother conceive me.

6 Behold, thou desirest truth in the inward parts: and in the hidden part thou shalt make me to know wisdom.

7 Purge me with hyssop, and I shall be clean: wash me, and I shall be whiter than snow.

8 Make me to hear joy and gladness; that the bones which thou hast broken may rejoice.

9 Hide thy face from my sins, and blot out all mine iniquities.

10 Create in me a clean heart, O God; and renew a right spirit within me.

11 Cast me not away from thy presence; and take not thy Holy Spirit from me.

12 Restore unto me the joy of thy salvation; and uphold me with thy free Spirit.

13 Then will I teach transgressors thy ways; and sinners shall be converted unto thee.

14 Deliver me from bloodguiltiness, O God, thou God of my salvation: and my tongue shall sing aloud of thy righteousness.

15 O Lord, open thou my lips; and my mouth shall shew forth thy praise.

16 For thou desirest not sacrifice; else would I give it: thou delightest not in burnt offering.

17 The sacrifices of God are a broken spirit: a broken and a contrite heart, O God, thou wilt not despise.

18 Do good in thy good pleasure unto Zion: build thou the walls of Jerusalem.

Didactic:—

19 Then shalt thou be pleased with the sacrifices of righteousness, with burnt offering and whole burnt offering: then shall they offer bullocks upon thine altar.

The didactic verses in the 148th Psalm are the fifth and sixth. These verses should be brought in contrast with the rest to make the distinction obvious.

§ 10.—SARCASM.

When we are in earnest we use upward ╱ and downward ╲ inflections; in "sarcasm," on the contrary, we do not mean our words *just as they are;* the sarcastic expression is obtained by a *combination* of the upward ╱ and downward ╲ inflections, which will give us the circumflex ᴗ, and the downward ╲ and upward ╱, which will give us the circumflex ⌒; and these circumflexes alternated and adjoined will give the "sarcastic" expression or intonation to our words, ⌒ ᴗ ⌒ ᴗ.

Example from Cowper on "Conversation":

    * * *   Vociferated logic kills me quite,
A noisy man is always in the right,
'Tis the most asinine employ on earth

To hear them tell of parentage and birth,
And echo conversations dull and dry,
Embellished with " he said " and "so said I."
* * * * * *
I pity bashful men who feel the pain
Of fancied scorn and undeserved disdain,
And bear the marks upon a blushing face
Of needless shame, and self-imposed disgrace.
Our sensibilities are so acute,
The fear of [being silent], makes us mute.
True modesty is a *discerning* grace,
And only blushes in the *proper* place ;
But counterfeit is blind, and skulks through fear,
Where 'tis a shame to be ashamed to appear ;
Humility the parent of the first,
The last by vanity produced and nursed.
* * * * * *
We next inquire, but softly and by stealth,
Like conservators of the public health,
Of epidemic throats, if such there are,
And coughs and rheums and phthisics and catarrh.

Here is another example of sarcasm from Merchant of Venice, Act 1, Sc. 3:

Shy. Signior Antonio, many a time and oft,
In the Rialto you have rated me
About my monies, and my usances :
Still have I borne it with a patient shrug ;
For *sufferance* is the badge of all our tribe:
You call me—misbeliever, cut-throat dog,

And spit upon my Jewish gaberdine,
And all for use of that which is mine *own.*
Well, then, it now appears, you need my *help:*
Go to then; you come to me, and you say,
"Shylock, we would have *monies*"; *You* say so:

HATE. { You, that did void your rheum upon my beard,
And foot me, as you spurn a stranger cur
Over your threshold; monies is your suit.

What should I say to you? Should I not say,
Hath a dog money? is it possible,
A cur can lend three thousand ducats; or
Shall I bend low, and in a bondman's key,
With 'bated breath, and whispering humbleness,
Say this,——
Fair sir, you spit on me on Wednesday last,
You spurn'd me such a day; another time
You call'd me—dog; and for these courtesies
I'll lend you thus much monies.

Shylock does not mean the words "just as they stand"; he means, in fact, that he should say the opposite of "Fair sir," etc., and by combining the circumflexes we have exactly the intonation of sarcasm.

Scorn takes the double circumflex, but with more *force* than sarcasm, and a considerable measure of the "aspirate"—as when Lady Macbeth says:

"My hands are of your colour!
But I shame to wear a heart so white!"

The "sneer" is also given with the double circumflex,

but without force, and only a slightly aspirated tone; as when in the same play Lady M. says:

> "What beast was't then,
> That made you break this enterprise to me?
> When you durst do it, then you were a man:
> And, to be more than what you were, you would
> Be so much more the man."

As she goes on farther in the same speech, the sneer merges into "anger," which requires abrupt force to give it due expression. Irony is neither so bitter nor so strong as sarcasm, so that the "ironical," which usually expresses censure in the language of praise, takes the undulations of tone peculiar to sarcasm; but these tones belie the words and pleased expression of face. Irony takes less "force" than sarcasm. The "wave" of the voice is less in "contempt," but the aspirate is infinitely more powerful.

The following is an illustration of varied intonations, scorn, contempt and sarcasm being the principal; from *Julius Cæsar*, Act I, Sc. 2:

(*Flourish and shout.*)

Bru. What means this shouting? I do fear, the people
Choose Cæsar for their king.
   Cas. Ay, do you *fear* it?
Then must I think you would not *have* it so.
   Bru. I would not, Cassius; yet I love him well:—
But wherefore do you hold me here so long?
What is it that you would impart to me?
If it be aught toward the general good,

Set honour in one eye, and death i' the other,
And I will look on both indifferently :
For, let the gods so speed me, as I love
The name of honour more than I fear death.

Cas. I know that virtue to be in you, Brutus,
As well as I do know your outward favour.
Well, [*honour*] is the subject of my story.—
I cannot tell, what you and other men
Think of this life ; but, for my single self,
I had as lief *not* be, as live to be
In *awe* of such a thing as *I* myself.
I was born as free as *Cæsar;* so were *you:*
We both have fed as well ; and we can both
Endure the winter's cold, as well as he.
For once, upon a raw and gusty day,
The troubled Tiber chafing with her shores,
Cæsar said to me, Dar'st thou, Cassius, now
Leap in with me into this angry flood,
And swim to yonder point ?—Upon the word,
Accouter'd as I was, I plunged in,
And bade him follow : so, indeed, he did.
The torrent roar'd ; and we did buffet it
With lusty sinews ; throwing it aside
And stemming it with hearts of controversy.
But ere we could arrive the point proposed,
Cæsar cried, Help me, Cassius, or I sink.
I, as Æneas, our great ancestor,
Did from the flames of Troy upon his shoulder
The old Anchises bear, so, from the waves of Tiber
Did I the tired Cæsar : And this man
Is now become [a god]; and Cassius is

A wretched creature, and must bend his body,
If Cæsar carelessly but nod on him.
He had a fever when he was in Spain,
And, when the fit was on him, I did mark
How he did shake: 'tis true, this god did shake:
His coward lips did from their colour fly;
And that same eye, whose bend doth awe the world,
Did lose his lustre: I did hear him groan:
Ay, and that tongue of his, that bade the Romans
Mark him, and write his speeches in their books,
Alas! it cried, [Give me some drink, Titinius],
As a sick girl. Ye gods, it doth amaze me,
A man of such a feeble temper should
So get the *start* of the majestic world,
And bear the palm *alone*. (*Shout. Flourish.*)

Bru. Another general shout!
I do believe, that these applauses are
For some new honours that are heap'd on Cæsar.

Cas. Why, man, he doth bestride the narrow world,
Like a Colossus; and we petty men
Walk under his huge legs, and peep about
To find ourselves dishonourable graves.
Men at some time are masters of their fates:
The fault, dear Brutus, is not in our stars,
But in ourselves, that we are uuderlings.
Brutus, and Cæsar: What should be in that Cæsar?
Why should that name be sounded more than yours?
Write them together, yours is as fair a name;
Sound them, it doth become the mouth as well;
Weigh them, it is as heavy; *conjure* with them,
Brutus will start a spirit as soon as Cæsar. (*Shout.*)

Now in the names of all the gods at once,
Upon what meat doth this our Cæsar feed,
That he is grown so great? Age thou art ashamed
Rome, thou hast *lost* the breed of noble bloods!
When went there by an age, since the great flood,
But it was famed with more than with one man?
When could they say, till now, that talk'd of Rome,
That her wide walks encompass'd but [one man]?
Now is it Rome indeed, and room enough,
When there is in it but one only man.
O! you and I have heard our fathers say,
There was a Brutus once, that would have brook'd
The eternal devil to keep his state in Rome,
As easily as a king.

Bru. That you do love me, I am nothing jealous;
What you would work me to, I have some aim:
How I have thought of this, and of these times,
I shall recount *hereafter;* for this present,
I would not, so with love I might entreat you,
Be any *farther* moved. What you have said,
I will *consider;* what you *have* to say,
I will with patience *hear:* and find a time
Both meet to hear, and answer, such high things,
Till then, my noble friend, chew upon this;
Brutus had rather be a villager,
Then to repute himself a son of Rome
Under these hard conditions as this time
Is like to *lay* upon us.

Cas. I am glad that my weak words
Have struck but thus much shew of fire from Brutus.

§ 11.—THE THROAT VOICE.

This is the sign of execration, disgust, aversion. This guttural intonation is caused by a drawing back of the tongue, and a closing of the pharynx, producing those harsh vibrations which are heard in the expression of the above-named emotions. In practising the exercises given for the acquirement of facility in rendering passages which need the throat voice, the student will give great prominence to all the consonants; especially "c" (having the sound of "k"), "r," "t," and "d."

Examples:

You common cry of curs ! whose breath I hate,
As reek o' the rotten fens, whose loves I prize
As the dead carcases of unburied men
That do corrupt my air, I banish you ;
And here remain, with your uncertainty !
—*Coriolanus.*

CHAPTER VI.

GESTURE.

WITH the Romans "*Actio*" comprised the general delivery, or what is now called *Elocution;* "*Elocutio*"—the choice of words or diction. Dr. Blair translates "*Actio*" as delivery.

It has been erroneously said that " Gestures should not be practised," but that "if the speaker be in

words in the minds of his audience. Therefore I would enforce upon students of elocution the necessity of practising gesture. The involuntary gestures which they afterwards make, in excitement perhaps, will often be very different from those which they have practised, yet even these will have been immeasurably improved.

The movement should as a usual thing proceed from the *superior* part of the body—that is, from the shoulder, not the elbow; from the thigh, not the knee;

from the knuckle, not the finger-joint; else the gestures will be extremely awkward, angular, and ungraceful.

Generally, voice, features and limbs should simultaneously express the same passion and thought. In ill-suppressed feeling, etc., however, the gestures will precede the voice.

Decision of action is more important than grace. The most ungraceful action, if decided, will be more effective than the most graceful without decision. Study repose. Observe the manner in which passions and emotions are expressed in real life. When you attempt to express any passion by gesture, inspire yourself with that secondary kind of feeling, which the imagination is capable of exciting, and then follow feeling with this observance, that you "o'erstep not the modesty of nature."

The language of gesture is not confined to the more vehement passions. Upon every subject and occasion on which we speak, some kind of "feeling" accompanies the words, and this feeling has always its appropriate gesture. I would advise my readers to observe the attitudes and actions in paintings and sculpture; also those of actors and orators. Practice attitudes and actions by themselves without words—just as a vocalist studies vocal expression apart from songs, or a danseuse, steps and figures apart from the dance, of which they form a part. Cicero says, that "those who have learned at the Palæstra are distinguished, even in other exercises, by their grace and agility; they who have learned to dance elegantly are also easily distinguished in all their motions from the untaught, even when they are not dancing. And the gesture also of the well-instructed speaker, even in its most trivial movements, is altogether different from neglected rudeness.

In all the parts of general discourse that turn upon mere reasoning, or when precision in stating mere doctrinal arguments is necessary, the simply intellectual style of gesture and delivery may be used. Propriety is the essence of real oratorical grace.

If vehemence be used in trifles, solemnity upon commonplace, pathos where there is nothing interesting, or dignity displayed where there is none in the sentiment, the result is affectation, which will impose only upon the ignorant; on the thoughtful mind the effect is such as the profligate produces when he descants on piety, or the coward on valor.

Abrupt, short and angular actions, if they bear the stamp of truth, are proper, as those of an old man under irritation; and, if ill applied, the most flowing and beautiful motions, the finest transitions of gesture, will become indecorous or offensive. In writing, even an appropriate term must not be used too frequently, and in this art the same action must not be too frequent. Aim at variety.

Gestures may be divided into intentional and unintentional, natural and artificial movements. A third class of gestures are termed "complex."

1. Natural or unintentional movements; as, a change of color produced by shame, or trembling occasioned by fear.

2. Intentional or artificial gestures; as, the finger on the lips to enjoin silence, the figure drawn upward in pride, the arm extended in authority.

3. Complex gestures formed by the combination of simple gestures; as, in "terror," the person will seek to escape the cause of fear—should it be a lion, by the foot extended to run, the hands held out to avoid obstacles which might impede, the head turned back to watch if the animal be in pursuit.

SIMPLE INTENTIONAL OR ARTIFICIAL GESTURES.

The Head.

To hang down the head implies "shame."
To hold it up, "valor," "pride."
To toss it back, "disagreement."
A forward inclination, "bashfulness."
A forward nod, "assent."
The head averted, "antipathy," horror."
The head leans forward in earnest attention.

The Eyes

Weep in "sorrow."
Burn or flash in "anger."
Are downcast or turned away in "displeasure."
Raised in "prayer" and "supplication."
Look on vacancy in "thought."
Are cast about in different directions in "doubt" or "mental trouble."

The Arms

Are spread, extended or elevated in "admiration."
Held forward, when "imploring."
They drop suddenly in "disappointment" or "despair."
An arm is held straight before the person in "authority."

The Hands.

The hand on the head denotes "suffering."
The hand on the eyes, "confusion."
The hand on the lips desires "silence."
The hand on the breast indicates "hope," and also appeals to conscience.
The hand waved or shaken, "joy" and "disdain."
The hands are clasped in "prayer."
The hands descend with palm down in "blessing."
The hands are wrung in "affliction."
The hands held forward, palm up, in "friendship."

The Body.

An upright carriage denotes "courage."
Held backward, "self-importance."
Inclined forward, "compassion," "courtesy."
Bent, "reverence."
Prostrated in "extreme humility."

The Limbs.

In an immovable position, "determination."
Knees bent in "timidity."

When moved uneasily, "mental disturbance."
They advance in "expectation."
Retire in "fear."
Start in "fright."
Stamp in "rage."
Kneel in "prayer."

COMPLEX GESTURES.

Terror.

The first impulse of one who suffers under this passion is to avoid or fly from the object feared. Suppose it to be a rattlesnake, on which he has almost trodden: he starts back, and looks downward. If the danger is in the distance, the figure should be represented looking forward, not starting backward, but slowly retiring, as if taking time to decide upon a plan of action.

Aversion.

The hand (vertical) is turned back towards the face; the eyes and head are eagerly directed to the object for an instant, the feet take a step forward; suddenly the head is averted, the arms are extended toward the object, hands vertical, feet retired.

Horror

is a combination of the two passions, whose signs have just been described. It transfixes the person, rendering him incapable of a retreat; the eyes are riveted on the object; the arm is extended, hand vertical; trembling seizes the body.

Admiration.

If of natural objects that are pleasing, the hands are held across each other, vertical palms across the breast (curve lines), and are then moved slowly outward, face smiling; if the emotion is aroused by unlooked-for or wonderful circumstances, the arms are suddenly elevated, palms supine; eyes and face are turned upwards at the same moment.

Listening,

which is eager for quick and sure information, presents a keen glance of the eye in the direction of the sounds; if nothing is revealed the ear is turned to the point of interest, the eye bent on space—this is instantaneous; the hand and arm are held vertical and extended, in a contrary direction, as if to keep off anything or anybody from interfering to drown the sounds. If the sounds proceed from different places, the arms are elevated, and the head moves from side to side—rapidly if alarmed, slowly if pleased; the reason being that when pleased we leave one sound to attend to another with regret; if frightened, we cannot endure to dwell long on the sounds that occasion the emotion.

Veneration

bows the head, casts down the eyes, crosses the hands on the breast, movements slow. Awe is supposed to deprive one of the power of quick volition.

Deprecation,

when extreme, sinks on one knee, clasps the hands tightly, throws the head back between the shoulders, and looks eagerly into the face of the one implored.

Shame

sinks on one knee, covering the eyes with the hands; if not so extreme, hangs the head.

Resignation

falls on the knee, crosses the arms on the breast, looks up towards heaven slowly.

Desperate Resignation.

The body upright, the head thrown back, the eyes fixed, the arms folded.

An Appeal to Heaven.

First place the right hand on the breast, then elevate the left arm palm upwards, the eyes look forward, then up to heaven.

An Appeal to Conscience.

The right hand is placed on the breast, the left arm falls to the side, the eyes look steadily at the person addressed.

Grief.

When the news of unexpected affliction is heard, the eyes are covered with the right hand, to shut out the "sight" which the speaker calls up, a step forward, the psychological impulse being to escape from the trouble, which thought, causes involuntary movement in an opposite direction; the left hand is thrown back, the mental impulse being "I can bear no more," and occasions the corresponding physical action, of putting back or away from one.

Attention,

when deeply interested, places the finger on the lips; the body takes a forward inclination; quiet is urged with the other hand.

Sudden Pain,

whether mental or physical, places the palm of the hand on the forehead, throws the body backward; these actions are accompanied by a long quick step in the same direction.

Reflection

holds the chin with the right hand, the left supports the elbow. Sometimes the back of the hands are placed on the waist, arms akimbo.

Pride,

in excess, elevates the head, straightens the figure, and places the elbow nearly forward akimbo.

There are three great classes of gesture (comic gesticulations would make a fourth):

1. The Heroic.

This accompanies descriptions of the majestic; the

utterance of noble or sublime thoughts; wherever the orotund quality of voice is appropriately applied; one who exercises this class of gesture in perfection should possess every natural and cultivated ability.

2. The Oratorical.

Precision, energy, and variety distinguish the gestures of a great orator; they are of more importance to him than "grace," for, while the latter is seldom absent in the actions of an accomplished speaker, the former are of vital necessity. Gestures of this class are employed in the delivery of sermons, lectures, arguments, speeches.

3. The Conversational.

This is employed in what is called "light comedy," dialogues, colloquies, in polite society, etc. Variety, grace, and simplicity are the characteristics of this class, and the movements are more lightly executed than those of the two classes discussed above.

ORDERS OF THE FIRST CLASS.

1. *Grandeur.* — The arm and hand are swept through space with majesty and freedom; the centre of motion is the shoulder; the actions should be on a large scale, and commence with a graceful sweep, or curve line; the changes should be made without effort, and other movements or inclinations of the body or limbs should harmonize with the main action; the limbs should move with moderately long steps, with firmness and power.

The opposite of "grandeur" is indicated by abrupt,

constrained gesture, stiffness of the joints, and a fixed attitude of the body, uncertain movements, and short steps.

2. *Fearlessness.*—A thorough confidence in and knowledge of one's power, will venture any action or attitude, which will be striking in effect, however novel. Unexpected situations and changes create wonder and pleasure by their newness and grace, and so enforce the thoughts they represent with marked success.

The antithesis of "fearlessness" is "timidity," which desires but does not act boldly, is dubious as to its capabilities, and hesitating.

ORDERS OF THE SECOND CLASS.

1. *Precision* requires exactness of action, neatness. Like distinctness in utterance, gestures should be cleanly cut, and used at the precise moment with the identical word which calls for them.

The opposite would be indecision, vague or confused gestures employed indiscriminately; they serve rather to render doubtful the speaker's meaning, instead of giving point to his words.

2. *Energy* requires firmness, decided, straight, direct lines. The emphasis is greatly aided by energetic gesture.

The opposite is weakness and uncertainty.

3. *Variety* is easily acquired by those who have a facility in adapting fitting and different gestures to each thought and position. The study of "variety"

will banish the tendency to frequent repetition of favorite gestures.

The opposite is monotony, which is as fatal to gesture as to intonation.

ORDERS OF THE THIRD CLASS.

1. *Variety.*—The same as described previously.

2. *Simplicity* in gesture appears the natural result of the situation or feelings expressed; it neither exceeds, nor falls below the just limit of the sentiment.

Its opposite is "affectation."

3. *Grace* is natural to some, and may be acquired by the many through practice. Sufficient practice on the flowing curve-lines of grace give a confidence in one's ability, which gives to self-possessed dignity beautiful, agreeable gestures.

The practice of graceful gestures is confined to those exhibited in the best models of painting and sculpture, and in accordance with correct taste.

The opposites are ungainliness, vulgarity, brusqueness.

4. *Propriety* in gesture is the judicious use of those actions best adapted to illustrate the thought. It arises from the just perception, the proper weighing, and careful timing of the action, which is neither too much abridged, nor too floridly displayed.

The antithesis or negative of propriety is impropriety, contrary gestures.

In conversational gesture the elbow instead of the shoulder becomes the centre of motion. The action is made short and sharp by the hand, the fingers and wrist, instead of the long, flowing lines which the arm executes in heroic gesture.

NATURAL PRINCIPLES IN GESTURE.

Grace is expressed by "relaxation" curves, "curve-lines." In the balcony scene between Romeo and Juliet, these graceful curve-lines, whether of the finger, the hand, the arm, the inclination of the body, are used throughout; therefore I insert this scene for practice of gestures of this description; the pupils should take alternate sentences, or rather speeches, and while delivering them slowly, be required to make appropriate graceful gestures, which are all to be made up of " curves."

Act 2, Scene 2.

Romeo. "He jests at scars that never felt a wound,
   (*Juliet appears above at a window.*)
But soft, what light through yonder window breaks!
It is the east, and Juliet is the sun !—
Arise, fair sun, and kill the envious moon,
Who is already sick and pale with grief,
That thou her maid art far more fair than she :
Be not her maid, since she is envious ;
Her vestal livery is but sick and green,
And none but fools do wear it ; cast it off.—
It is my lady ; O, it is my love.
O, that she knew she were !—
She speaks, yet she says nothing ; What of that ?
Her eye discourses, I will answer it.—

I am too bold, 'tis not to me she speaks:
Two of the fairest stars in all the heaven,
Having some business, do entreat her eyes
To twinkle in their spheres till they return.
What if her eyes were there, they in her head?
The brightness of her cheek would shame those stars,
As daylight doth a lamp; her eye in heaven
Would through the airy region stream so bright,
That birds would sing, and think it were not night.
See how she leans her cheek upon her hand!
O, that I were a glove upon that hand,
That I might touch that cheek!

Jul. Ah me!

Rom. She speaks:—
O, speak again, bright angel! for thou art
As glorious to this night, being o'er my head,
As is a winged messenger of heaven
Unto the white-upturned wond'ring eyes
Of mortals, that fall back to gaze on him,
When he bestrides the lazy-pacing clouds,
And sails upon the bosom of the air.

Jul. O Romeo, Romeo! wherefore art thou Romeo?
Deny thy father, and refuse thy name:
Or, if thou wilt not, be but sworn my love,
And I'll no longer be a Capulet.

Rom. Shall I hear more, or shall I speak at this?
(*Aside.*)

Jul. 'Tis but thy name, that is my enemy;—
Thou art thyself, though not a Montague.
What's Montague? it is nor hand, nor foot,
Nor arm, nor face, nor any other part
Belonging to a man. O, be some other name!
What's in a name? that, which we call a rose,

By any other name would smell as sweet;
So Romeo would, where he not Romeo call'd,
Retain that dear perfection which he owes,
Without that title:—Romeo, doff thy name;
And for that name, which is no part of thee,
Take all myself.

Rom. I take thee at thy word:
Call me but love, and I'll be new baptized!
Henceforth I never will be Romeo.

Jul. What man art thou, that, thus bescreen'd in night,
So stumblest on my counsel?

Rom. By a name
I know not how to tell thee who I am:
My name, dear saint, is hateful to myself,
Because it is an enemy to thee;
Had I it written, I would tear the word.

Jul. My ears have not yet drunk a hundred words
Of that tongue's utterance, yet I know the sound:
Art thou not Romeo, and a Montague?

Rom. Neither, fair saint, if either thee dislike.

Jul. How camest thou hither? tell me, and wherefore?
The orchard walls are high, and hard to climb;
And the place death, considering who thou art,
If any of my kinsmen find thee here.

Rom. With love's light wings did I o'er-perch these walls:
For stony limits cannot hold love out:
And what love can do, that dares love attempt;
Therefore thy kinsmen are no let to me.

Jul. If they do see thee, they will murder thee.

Rom. Alack! there lies more peril in thine eye,

Than twenty of their swords; look thou but sweet,
And I am proof against their enmity.
   Jul. I would not for the world they saw thee here.
   Rom. I have night's cloak to hide me from their sight;
And, but thou love me, let them find me here:
My life was better ended by their hate,
Than death prorogued, wanting of thy love.
   Jul. By whose direction found'st thou out this place?
   Rom. By love, who first did prompt me to inquire;
He lent me counsel, and I lent him eyes.
I am no pilot; yet wert thou as far
As that vast shore wash'd with the farthest sea,
I would adventure for such merchandise.
   Jul. Thou know'st the mask of night is on my face;
Else would a maiden blush bepaint my cheek,
For that which thou hast heard me speak to-night
Fain would I dwell on form, fain, fain deny
What I have spoke; but farewell compliment!
Dost love me? I know, thou wilt say—Ay;
And I will take thy word: yet, if thou swear'st
Thou mayst prove false; at lovers' perjuries,
They say, Jove laughs. O gentle Romeo,
If thou dost love, pronounce it faithfully:
Or if thou think'st I am too quickly won,
I'll frown and be perverse, and say thee nay,
So thou wilt woo; but, else, not for the world.
In truth, fair Montague, I am too fond;
And therefore thou mayst think my haviour light:
But trust me, gentleman, I'll prove more true
Than those that have more cunning to be strange.
I should have been more strange, I must confess,
But that thou overheard'st, ere I was ware,

My true love's passion: therefore pardon me;
And not impute this yielding to light love,
Which the dark night hath so discovered.

Rom. Lady, by yonder blessed moon I swear,
That tips with silver all these fruit-tree tops,—

Jul. O, swear not by the moon, the inconstant moon,
That monthly changes in her circled orb,
Lest that thy love prove likewise variable.

Rom. What shall I swear by?

Jul. Do not swear at all;
Or, if thou wilt, swear by thy gracious self,
Which is the god of my idolatry,
And I'll believe thee.

Rom. If my heart's dear love—

Jul. Well, do not swear: although I joy in thee,
I have no joy of this contract to-night:
It is too rash, too unadvised, too sudden;
Too like the lightning, which doth cease to be,
Ere one can say—It lightens. Sweet, good night!
This bud of love, by summer's ripening breath,
May prove a beauteous flower when next we meet.
Good night, good night! as sweet repose and rest
Come to thy heart, as that within my breast!

Rom. O, wilt thou leave me so unsatisfied?

Jul. What satisfaction canst thou have to-night?

Rom. The exchange of thy love's faithful vow for mine.

Jul. I gave thee mine before thou didst request it:
And yet I would it were to give again.

Rom. Wouldst thou withdraw it? for what purpose, love?

Jul. But to be frank, and give it thee again.
And yet I wish but for the thing I have:

My bounty is as boundless as the sea,
My love as deep; the more I give to thee,
The more I have, for both are infinite.—
(Nurse calls within.)
I hear some noise within: Dear love, adieu!—
Anon, good nurse!—Sweet Montague, be true.
Stay, but a little, I will come again.

Energy is expressed by tenseness; *straight direct lines.*

Beat. Sweet Hero!—she is wronged, she is slandered, she is undone.
Bene. Beat—
Beat. Princes and counties! Surely, a princely testimony, a goodly count-confect; a sweet gallant, surely! O, that I were a man for his sake! or that I had any friend would be a man for my sake! But manhood is melted into courtesies, valor into compliment, and men are only turned into tongue, and trim ones too: he is now as valiant as Hercules, that only tells a lie, and swears it.—I cannot be a man with wishing, therefore I will die a woman with grieving.
—*Much Ado about Nothing*, Act 4, Sc. 1.

Beatrice uses here the straight lines natural in expressing energetic thought; curve-lines would *belie* the emotion with which Beatrice is filled, when warmly taking the part of her friend Hero.

Affirmative.—In these gestures the hand is supine (or palm uppermost); if the facts or thoughts affirmed be of the "graceful" order (sentiments that express tenderness, affection, beauty of thought), curve-lines are employed, if the thoughts be "energetic," as in manifestations of pride, anger, excessive joy, etc., etc., these curves give place to straight lines; for the first order, I give a passage from the Merchant of Venice, as an examplification;—Portia's speech;—in Shylock's reply, gestures of the second order are employed, and in Bassanio *eagerness* in tendering the ducats; the same straight lines are necessary; in the concluding lines from Portia "negative" gestures are predominant.

Por. The quality of mercy is not strain'd;
It droppeth, as the gentle rain from heaven,
Upon the place beneath; it is twice bless'd,—
It blesseth him that gives, and him that takes.
'Tis mightiest in the mightiest: it becomes
The throned monarch better than his crown;
His sceptre shews the force of temporal power,
The attribute to awe and majesty,
Wherein doth sit the dread and fear of kings;
But mercy is above this sceptred sway,
It is enthroned in the hearts of kings,
It is an attribute to God himself;
And earthly power doth then shew likest God's
When mercy seasons justice. Therefore, Jew,
Though justice be thy plea, consider this,—
That in the course of justice, none of us
Should see salvation: we do pray for mercy;
And that same prayer doth teach us all to render
The deeds of mercy. I have spoke thus much
To mitigate the justice of thy plea;
Which if thou follow, this strict court of Venice
Must needs give sentence 'gainst the merchant there.

Shy. My deeds upon my head! I crave the law,
The penalty and forfeit of my bond.

Por. Is he not able to discharge the money?

Bass. Yes, here I tender it for him in the court;
Yea, twice the sum : if that will not suffice,
I will be bound to pay it ten times o'er,
On forfeit of my hands, my head, my heart,
If this will not suffice, it must appear,
That malice bears down truth. And I beseech you,
Wrest once the law to your authority :
To do a great right, do a little wrong;
And curb this cruel devil of his will.

Por. It must not be ; there is no power in Venice
Can alter a decree established ;
'Twill be recorded for a precedent :
And many an error, by the same example,
Will rush into the state : it cannot be.

Negative.—This is expressed by the hand prone (or palm downward); if the negative be regretfully given, or the reproof be gentle, the negative gestures will partake more or less of the curved line, and the time be slower in giving them ; but if the thoughts, which prompt negative gestures, be awe-inspiring, the result of horror, or of shame, etc., straight lines given in rather faster time are necessary. I give an example for practice from "Measure for Measure"; the first lines as far as "pendent world" belonging to the first of these orders; and afterwards the action grows more and more energetic and negative, except at the words "is a paradise," where elevation of hands is required, and strong negative on the last line :—

Claud. Ay, but to die, and go we not know where;
To lie in cold obstruction, and to rot;
This sensible warm motion to become
A kneaded clod; and the delighted spirit
To bathe in fiery floods, or to reside
In thrilling regions of thick-ribbed ice;
To be imprison'd in the viewless winds.
And blown with restless violence round about
The pendent world; or to be worse than worst
Of those, that lawless and uncertain thoughts
Imagine howling!—'tis too horrible!
The weariest and most loathed worldly life,
That age, ache, penury, and imprisonment
Can lay on nature, is a paradise
To what we fear of death.
—*Measure for Measure.*

Acceptation.—Here the hand or hands are supine, the gestures direct but not energetic, they must not lose a certain grace; the lines being not too much curved, nor yet too straight.

Ant. I have heard,
Your grace hath ta'en great pains to qualify
His rigorous course; but since he stands obdurate,
And that no lawful means can carry me
Out of his envy's reach, I do oppose
My patience to his fury, and am arm'd
To suffer, with a quietness of spirit,
The very tyranny and rage of his.
—*Merchant of Venice.*

This also from *Antony and Cleopatra*, Act 2, Sc. 5:

Re-enter IRAS, *with a robe, crown, &c.*

Cleo. Give me my robe, put on my crown; I have
Immortal longings in me: Now no more
The juice of Egypt's grape shall moist this lip :—
Yare, yare, good Iras; quick.—Methinks I hear
Antony call; I see him rouse himself
To praise my noble act; I hear him mock
The luck of Cæsar, which the gods give men
To excuse their after wrath: Husband, I come:
Now to that name my courage prove my title!
I am fire and air; my other elements
I give to baser life.—So,—have you done?
Come, then, and take the last warmth of my lips.
Farewell, kind Charmian!—Iras, long farewell!

Common Gestures.—These are most emphatic on the horizontal line, but do not *repeat* the gesture on the same emphasis.

Example from *Julius Cæsar*, Act 4, Sc. 1:

Bru. No, not an oath: if not the face of men,
The sufferance of our souls, the time's abuse,—
If these be motives weak, break off betimes,
And every man hence to his idle bed;
So let high-sighted tyranny rage on,
Till each man drop by lottery. But if these,
As I am sure they do, bear fire enough
To kindle cowards, and to steel with valour
The melting spirits of women; then, countrymen,
What need we any spur, but our own cause,

A declarative interrogative.

To prick us to redress? what other bond,
Than secret *Romans*, that have spoke the word,
And will not palter? and what other oath,
Than honesty to honesty engaged.
That *this* shall be, or we will fall for it?
Swear priests, and cowards, and [men cautelous],
Old feeble carrions, and [such suffering souls
That welcome *wrongs*]; unto bad causes swear
Such creatures as men doubt: but do not stain
The even virtue of our enterprise,
Nor the insuppressive mettle of our spirits,
To think, that, or our cause, or our performance,
Did need an oath; when every drop of blood,
That every Roman bears, and nobly bears,
Is guilty of a several bastardy,
If he do break the smallest particle
Of any *promise* that hath pass'd from him.

Rejection.—Gestures which *precede* the words of rejection are improper; these actions should immediately follow the word.

Example:

P. Hen. I *never* thought to hear you speak *again.*
K. Hen. Thy *wish* was *father*, Harry, to that
    thought;
I stay too long by thee, I weary thee.
Dost thou so hunger for my empty chair,

That thou wilt needs invest thee with mine honours,
Before thy hour be ripe? O foolish youth!
Thou seek'st the greatness that will overwhelm thee.
—*Henry IV*, Part 2.

In this speech of Viola's from *Twelfth Night* most of the gestures are those of rejection; others are of "negation," and the pupil will distribute his gestures according to the sentiments expressed:

Vio. I left no ring with her: What means this
    lady?
Fortune forbid, my outside have not charm'd her!
She made good view of me; indeed, so much,
That, sure, methought, her eyes had lost her tongue,
For she did speak in starts distractedly.
She loves me, sure; the cunning of her passion
Invites me in this churlish messenger.
None of my lord's ring! why, he sent her none.
I am the man,—If it be so, (as 'tis,)
Poor lady, she were better love a dream.
Disguise, I see, thou art a wickedness,
Wherein the pregnant enemy does much.
How easy is it for the proper-false
In women's waxen hearts to set their forms!
Alas, our frailty is the cause, not we;
For, such as we are made of, such we be;
How will this fadge? My master loves her dearly:
And I, poor monster, fond as much on him;
And she, mistaken, seems to dote on me:
What will become of this? As I am man
My state is desperate for my master's love;
As I am woman, now alas the day!

What thriftless sighs shall poor Olivia breathe?
O time, thou must untangle this, not I;
It is too hard a knot for me to untie.

Propulsion.—Gestures of this class are used in describing the supernatural, when fear or horror are accompanying emotions, also in fright of any real or imaginary object. The hand or hands are vertical in front of the breast, the fingers slightly separated, as endeavoring to ward or keep off the object feared.

Examples:

Macb. Avaunt! and quit my sight! Let the earth hide thee!
Thy bones are marrowless, thy blood is cold;
Thou hast no speculation in those eyes
Which thou dost glare with!
—*Macbeth.*

Brutus. * * * * *
I think it is the weakness of mine eyes,
That shapes this monstrous apparition.
It comes upon me:—Art thou any thing?
Art thou some god, some angel, or some devil,
That makest my blood cold, and my hair to stare?
Speak to me, what thou art.
Ghost. Thy evil spirit, Brutus.
—*Julius Cæsar.*

Juliet frequently uses these "propulsive" gestures throughout the sad scene in which she takes the poison, and acts her "dismal part alone":

La. Cap. Good night!
Get thee to bed, and rest; for thou hast need.

      [*Exeunt Lady Capulet and Nurse.*
Jul. Farewell!—God knows when we shall meet
  again.
I have a faint cold fear thrills through my veins,
That almost freezes up the heat of life :
I'll call them back again to comfort me ;—
Nurse! What should she do here?
My dismal scene I needs must act alone.—
Come, phial.—
What if this mixture do not work at all?
Must I of force be married to the county?—
No, no ;—this shall forbid it :—lie thou there.—
        [*Laying down a dagger.*
What if it be poison, which the friar
Subtly have minister'd to have me dead ;
Lest in this marriage he should be dishonour'd,
Because he married me before to Romeo.
I fear, it is : and yet, methinks, it should not,
For he hath still been tried a holy man :
I will not entertain so bad a thought.
How if, when I am laid into the tomb,
I wake before the time that Romeo
Come to redeem me? there's a fearful point!
Shall I not then be stifled in the vault,
To whose foul mouth no healthsome air breathes in,
And there die strangled ere my Romeo comes?
Or, if I live, is it not very like
The horrible conceit of death and night,
Together with the terror of the place,—
As in a vault, an ancient receptacle,
Where, for these many hundred years, the bones
Of all my buried ancestors are pack'd ;
Where bloody Tybalt, yet but green in earth,

Lies fest'ring in his shroud ; where, as they say,
At some hours in the night spirits resort ;—
Alack, alack ! is it not like, that I,
So early waking,—what with loathsome smells ;
And shrieks like mandrakes torn out of the earth,
That living mortals, hearing them, run mad ;—
O ! if I wake, shall I not be distraught,
Environed with all these hideous fears?
And madly play with my forefathers' joints ?
And pluck the mangled Tybalt from his shroud ?
And, in his rage, with some great kinsman's bone,
As with a club, dash out my desperate brains ?
O, look ! methinks I see my cousin's ghost
Seeking out Romeo, that did spit his body
Upon a rapier's point :—Stay, Tybalt, stay !—
Romeo, I come ! this do I drink to thee.

(*She throws herself upon the bed.*)

Gestures of rejection should frequently be employed, as if putting away from her the horrible images which her own mind has conjured ; these horrors render her nearly distraught with fear, and the hands occasionally clasping the head, the seat of reason, will signify the trouble that weighs there.

Pointing expresses *individuality*, or a special thought or object ; if an object is indicated, real or imaginary, the finger should be *prone;* if of a thought the finger should be supine. If the "thought" or object be of the energetic order use a straight line ; if of beauty or tenderness, etc., a curve line.

Here are two excellent examples from Macbeth. On "innocent flower" the gesture is on the curved line, but the other objects indicated are of the "energetic":

> *Lady M.* O, never
> Shall sun that morrow see!
> Your face, my thane, is as a book, where men
> May read strange matters.—To beguile the time,
> Look like the time: bear welcome in your eye,
> Your hand, your tongue: look like the innocent flower,
> But be the serpent under it. He that's coming
> Must be provided for: and you shall put
> This night's great business into my despatch;
> Which shall to all our nights and days to come
> Give solely sovereign sway and masterdom.
>
> * * * * * *
>
> *Por.* The crow doth sing as sweetly as the lark,
> When neither is attended; and, I think,
> The nightingale, if she should sing by day,
> When every goose is cackling, would be thought
> No better a musician than the wren.
> How many things by season season'd are
> To their right praise, and true perfection!—
> Peace, hoa! the moons sleeps with Endymion,
> And would not be awaked! (*Music ceases.*

Elevation of the hands expresses admiration and kindred sentiments, also praise to the Deity, and appeals to heaven.

Depression of the hands is expressive of sentiments the reverse of those which require the hands elevated: aversion, scorn, repulsion are among them. Also depression of the mind is so indicated.

Disgust and sorrow are also described by "depressed" hands.

Description.—In describing that which is disagreeable or repulsive it is natural to employ the horizontal line, but with the hand prone (or palm down); but in picturing the agreeable, the beautiful, use the horizontal line with the palm uppermost. Here is an example of the first order, taken from King Richard II:

K. Rich. No matter where; of comfort no man
    speak :
Let's talk of graves, of worms, and epitaphs ;
Make dust our paper, and with rainy eyes
Write sorrow on the bosom of the earth.
Let's choose executors, and talk of wills :
And yet not so,—for what can we bequeath,
Save our deposed bodies to the ground?
Our lands, our lives, and all are Bolingbroke's,
And nothing can we call our own, but death !
And that small model of the barren earth,
Which serve as paste and cover to our bones.
For Heaven's sake, let us sit upon the ground,
And tell sad stories of the death of kings :—
How some have been deposed, some slain in war ;
Some haunted by the ghosts they have deposed ;
Some poison'd by their wives, some sleeping kill'd :
All murder'd :—For within the hollow crown,
That rounds the mortal temples of a king,
Keeps death his court : and there the antic sits,
Scoffing his state, and grinning at his pomp ;
Allowing him a breath, a little scene

To monarchize, be fear'd, and kill with looks;
Infusing him with self and vain conceit,—
As if this flesh, which walls about our life,
Wore brass impregnable, and, humour'd thus,
Comes at the last, and with a little pin
Bores through his castle wall, and—farewell, king!
Cover your heads, and mock not flesh and blood
With solemn reverence; throw away respect,
Tradition, form, and ceremonious duty,
For you have but mistook me all this while;
I live with bread like you, feel want, taste grief,
Need friends :—Subjected thus,
How can you say to me—I am a king?

In the following speech of Antony's, he does not always mean the words just *as they are*, consequently the *gestures* are not meant just as they are given; the words are *fair* but the meaning is *sarcastic;* and naturally the gestures will exhibit a corresponding fairness, but a slight *exaggeration* of them will mark the sarcastic expression; they are mostly then on the "horizontal supine," somewhat exaggerated as I said before:

Ant. Good friends, sweet friends, let me not stir you up
To such a sudden flood of mutiny.
They, that have done this deed, are honourable;
What private griefs they have, alas, I know not,
That made them do it; they are wise and honourable,
And will, no doubt, with reasons answer you.
I come not, friends, to steal away your hearts;
I am no orator, as Brutus is;

> But, as you know me all, a plain blunt man,
> That love my friend: and that they know full well
> That gave me public leave to speak of him.
> For I have neither wit, nor words, nor worth,
> Action, nor utterance, nor the power of speech,
> To stir men's blood: I only speak right on;
> I tell you that, which you yoursèlves do know;
> Shew you sweet Cæsar's wounds, poor, poor dumb mouths,
> And bid them speak for me: But were I Brutus,
> And Brutus Antony, there were an Antony
> Would ruffle up your spirits, and put a tongue
> In every wound of Cæsar, that should move
> The stones of Rome to rise and mutiny.
> —*Julius Cæsar.*

Of the second order of descriptive gesture is this example from the *Midsummer Night's Dream*—the "horizontal line" must be employed, with hands supine:

> *Puck.* My fairy lord, this must be done with haste,
> For night's swift dragons cut the clouds full fast,
> And yonder shines Aurora's harbinger;
> At whose approach, ghosts, wandering here and there,
> Troop home to churchyards: damned spirits all,
> That in cross-ways and floods have burial,
> Already to their wormy beds are gone;
> For fear lest day should look their shames upon,
> They wilfully themselves exile from light,
> And must for aye consort with black-brow'd night.
>   *Obe.* But we are spirits of another sort:
> I with the morning's love have oft made sport;

And, like a forester, the groves may tread
Even till the eastern gate, all fiery red,
Opening on Neptune with far blessed beams,
Turns into yellow gold his salt-green streams.
But, notwithstanding, haste; make no delay:
We may effect this business yet ere day.
                                            [*Exit Ober.*]

* * * * * *

Obe. That very time I saw, (but thou couldst not,)
Flying between the cold moon and the earth,
Cupid all arm'd: a certain aim he took
At a fair vestal, throned by the west;
And loosed his love-shaft smartly from his bow,
As it should pierce a hundred thousand hearts;
But I might see young Cupid's fiery shaft
Quench'd in the chaste beams of the wat'ry moon;
And the imperial vot'ress passed on,
In maiden meditation, fancy free.
Yet mark'd I where the bolt of Cupid fell:
It fell upon a little western flower—
Before, milk-white; now, purple with love's wound,—
And maidens call it, love-in-idleness.
Fetch me that flower; the herb I shew'd thee once;
The juice of it on sleeping eyelids laid,
Will make or man or woman madly dote
Upon the next live creature that it sees.
Fetch me this herb; and be thou here again
Ere the leviathan can swim a league.

The action in the speeches of "Clarence's Dream," in King Richard III, is on the "horizontal prone," and sometimes, where the feeling is intense, and Clarence relates he dreamed he saw the murdered spirits who reproached him, propulsion is required as in the supernatural:

> *Brak.* What was your dream my lord? I pray you tell me.
> *Clar.* Methought that I had broken from the Tower,
> And was embark'd to cross to Burgundy;
> And, in my company, my brother Gloster;
> Who from my cabin tempted me to walk
> Upon the hatches, thence we look'd toward England,
> And cited up a thousand heavy times,
> During the wars of York and Lancaster,
> That had befallen us. As we paced along
> Upon the giddy footing of the hatches,
> Methought that Gloster stumbled; and, in falling,
> Struck me, that thought to stay him, overboard,
> Into the tumbling billows of the main,
> O Lord! methought what pain it was to drown!
> What dreadful noise of water in mine ears!
> What sights of ugly death within mine eyes!
> Methought I saw a thousand fearful wrecks;
> A thousand men, that fishes gnaw'd upon;
> Wedges of gold, great anchors, heaps of pearl,
> Inestimable stones, unvalued jewels,
> All scattered in the bottom of the sea,
> Some lay in dead men's skulls; and in those holes
> Where eyes did once inhabit, there were crept
> (As 'twere in scorn of eyes) reflecting gems,
> That woo'd the slimy bottom of the deep,
> And mock'd the dead bones that lay scatter'd by.
> *Brak.* Had you such leisure in the time of death,
> To gaze upon the secrets of the deep?

Clar. Methought I had, and often did I strive
To yield the ghost; but still the envious flood
Kept in my soul, and would not let it forth
To seek the empty, vast, and wand'ring air;
But smother'd it within my panting bulk,
Which almost burst to belch it in the sea.
  Brak. Awaked you not with this sore agony?
  Clar. O no, my dream was lengthen'd after life;
O, then began the tempest to my soul!
I pass'd, methought, the melancholy flood,
With that grim ferryman which poets write of,
Unto the kingdom of perpetual night.
The first that there did greet my stranger soul,
Was my great father-in-law, renowned Warwick;
Who cried aloud,— *What scourge for perjury
Can this dark monarchy afford false Clarence?*
And so he vanish'd: Then came wand'ring by
A shadow like an angel, with bright hair
Dabbled in blood: and he shriek'd out aloud,—
*Clarence is come,—false, fleeting, perjured Clarence,—
That stabb'd me in the field of Tewksbury;—
Seize on him, furies, take him to your torments!*
With that, methought, a legion of foul fiends
Environ'd me, and howl'd in mine ears
Such hideous cries, that, with the very noise,
I trembling waked, and, for a season after,
Could not believe but that I was in hell;
Such terrible impression made my dream.
  Brak. No marvel, lord, though it affrighted you;
I am afraid, methinks, to hear you tell it.
  Clar. O, Brakenbury, I have done these things—
That now give evidence against my soul—
For Edward's sake; and see how he requites me!—

O God! if my deep prayers cannot appease thee,
But thou wilt be avenged on my misdeeds,
Yet execute thy wrath on me alone:
O, spare my guiltless wife, and my poor children!—
I pray thee, gentle keeper, stay by me;
My soul is heavy, and I fain would sleep.

Extended hands are expressive of extent, of vastness, of multiplicity. The hands should never be extended behind the person, nor the *flat* hand be shown.

"Round he throws his baleful eyes
That witnessed huge affliction and dismay,
Mixed with obdurate pride and steadfast hate,
At once as far as angels ken he views
The dismal situation waste and wild:
A dungeon horrible, on all sides round,
As one great furnace flamed; yet from those flames
No light, but rather darkness visible,
Served only to discover sights of woe,
Regions of sorrow! doleful shades! where peace
And rest can never dwell! hope never comes
That comes to all: but torture without end
Still urges, and a fiery deluge fed
With ever-burning sulphur unconsumed!

Deferention.—The fingers are slightly separated—"as these flowers." An example from "Paradise Lost," Book 4, line 689:

"Thus talking, hand in hand alone they passed
On to their blissful bower: it was a place
Chosen by the sovereign when he framed

All things to man's delightful use ; the roof
Of thickest covert was inwoven shade
Laurel and myrtle ; and what higher grew,
Of firm and fragrant leaf : on either side
Acanthus, and each odorous bushy shrub,
Fenced up the verdant wall : each beauteous flower,
Iris all hues, roses, and jessamine,
Reared high their flourished heads between and wrought
Mosaic : underfoot the violet,
Crocus, and hyacinth, with rich inlay,
Broidered the ground."

CHAPTER VII.

MISCELLANEOUS EXAMPLES.

Emphasis:

> Who [reverenced his conscience] as his king:
> Whose glory was redressing human wrong,
> Who spake no slander,—no, nor listened to it,
> Who loved *one* only and who *clave* to her.
> —*Tennyson.*

Psychological positives and negatives:

> *Wolsey.* *Farewell*, a *long* farewell, to all my greatness!
> This is the [state of man]: To-day he puts forth
> The tender leaves of *hope*, to-morrow *blossoms*,
> And bears his [blushing honors] *thick* upon him:
> The third day comes a *frost*, a *killing* frost;
> And when he thinks (good easy man) full surely
> His greatness is a ripening—nips his root,
> And then he falls, as *I* do.
> —*Henry VIII.*, Act 3, Sc. 2.

Psy. pos. and neg.:

Lady M. Infirm of purpose! (*Pos. and neg.*)
Give *me* the daggers : the sleeping, and the dead,
Are but as pictures ;* 'tis the eye of childhood,
That fears a *painted* devil. If he do bleed, (*asp. as in secrecy*)
I'll gild the faces of the grooms withal,
For it must seem their guilt.
—*Macbeth.*

Psy. pos. and neg. :

Por. If to do were as *easy* as to know what were *good* to do, chapels had been churches, and poor men's cottages, princes' palaces. It is a good divine that *follows* his own instructions : I can easier teach *twenty* what were *good* to be done, than *be one* of the twenty to *follow* mine own teaching. The *brain* may devise *laws* for the blood ; but a hot temper leaps *over* a cold decree : such a *hare* is [madness the youth], to skip o'er the meshes of [good counsel the cripple]. But this reasoning is not in the fashion to choose me a *husband:*—O me, the word chóose! I may neither choose whom I would nor refuse whom I dislike ; so is the will of a living daughter curb'd by the will of a dead father :—Is it not hard, Nerissa, that I cannot choose one, nor refuse none?
—*Merchant of Venice,* Act 1, Sc. 2.

Here is an example from "Measure for Measure" of the positive and negative attitudes of mind of the

---

* Simile in quick time.

speakers with regard to the thoughts they express. The duke says, "Be absolute for *death*,"—make up your mind to die, and then in either event, whether *death* which it is natural to fear come, or *life* which is sweet, you will be resigned:—

Enter Duke, Claudio, and Provost.

Duke. So, then you hope of *pardon* from lord Angelo?

Claud. The *miserable* have no other *medicine*,
But only [*hope*]:
I have hope to *live*, and am prepared to *die*.

Duke. Be absolute for *death;* either *death*, or life,
Shall thereby be the *sweeter*. Reason *thus* with life,—
If I do *lose* thee, I do lose a thing
That none but fools would keep : a [*breath*] thou art,
(Servile to all the skyey influences,)
That dost this habitation, where thou keep'st,
Hourly *afflict:* merely, thou art death's fool;
For *him* thou labor'st by thy *flight* to shun,
And yet *runst* toward him still : Thou art *not* [*noble*];
For all the accommodations that thou bear'st,
Are nursed by baseness : Thou art by no means *valiant;*
For thou dost fear the soft and tender fork
Of a poor worm : Thy *best* of rest is *sleep*,
And that thou oft *provok'st;* yet grossly *fear'st*
Thy death, which is no more. Thou art *not* thyself;
For thou exist'st on many a thousand grains
That issue out of dust ; Happy thou *art not;*

For what thou hast not, still thou striv'st to get;
And what thou hast, forget'st. Thou art *not* certain;
For thy complexion shifts to strange effects,
After the moon: If thou art *rich*, thou art poor;
For, [like an ass, whose back with ingots bows],
Thou bear'st thy heavy riches but a journey,
And death unloads thee: *Friend* hast thou *none;*
For thine own bowels, which do call thee *sire*,
The mere effusion of thy proper loins,
Do curse the gout, serpigo, and the rheum,
For ending thee no sooner: Thou hast nor youth, nor age,
But, as it were, an [after-dinner's sleep],
Dreaming on *both;* for all thy blessed youth
Becomes as aged, and doth beg the arms
Of palsied eld; and when thou art old, and rich,
Thou hast neither heat, affection, limb, nor beauty,
To make thy riches *pleasant.* What's *yet* in this,
That bears the name of life? Yet in this life
Lie hid more thousand deaths: yet death we fear,
That makes these odds all *even.*

Claud. I humbly *thank* you.
To sue to *live*, I find, I seek to die;
And seeking death, find *life:* Let it come *on.*

An exercise on varied intonations from "As you like it":

Enter Rosalind, Celia, and Jacques.

Jaq. I pr'ythee, pretty youth, let me be better acquainted with thee.

Ros. They say you are a melancholy fellow.

Jaq. I am so : I do love it better than laughing.

Ros. Those, that are in extremity of either, are abominable fellows ; and betray themselves to every modern censure, worse than drunkards.

Jaq. Why, 'tis good to be sad and say nothing.

Ros. Why, then 'tis good to be a post.

Jaq. I have neither the scholar's melancholy, which is emulation ; nor the musician's, which is fantastical ; nor the courtier's, which is proud ; nor the soldier's, which is ambitious ; nor the lawyer's, which is politic ; nor the lady's which is nice ; nor the lover's, which is all these : but it is a melancholy of mine own, compounded of many simples, extracted from many objects ; and, indeed, the sundry contemplation of travels in which my often rumination wraps me, is a most humorous sadness.

Ros. A traveler ! By my faith, you have great reason to be sad : I fear, you have sold your own lands, to see other men's ; then, to have seen much, and to have nothing, is to have rich eyes and poor hands.

The practice of varied forms, simply in the requisition of the manner, will be the education of the ear, both for the purposes of " *accuracy* " and " *analysis.*"

The aspirate slightly given on " emulation " to denote *eagerness*, a *dwelling* on the vowel sounds in " fantastical," mark the *peculiarity*. On the next (proud), the <, which gives dignity, the frequent result of pride. Aspirate on " ambitious." Wave of the voice on " politic," to mark the lawyer's insinuating manner. Accent the consonants in " lady's " and " nice," to mark precision, " nattyness." Strong emphasis to " *all* " is speaking of the lover's melancholy.

This exercise requires a subdued semitone, as the sentiment is regretful and pleading; it is from "As you like it":

> " But whate'er you are
> That in this desert inaccessible
> (Under the shade of melancholy boughs)
> *Lose* and *neglect* the [creeping hours of time],
> If ever you have looked on *better* days,
> If ever been where *bells* have [knolled to church],
> If ever sat at any *good* man's feast,
> And know what 'tis to *pity* and be pitied,
> Let *gentleness* my *strong enforcement* be."

The next requires a nearly similar intonation—"Ingratitude":

> Blow, blow, thou wintry wind,
> Thou art not so unkind
>   As man's ingratitude;
> Thy tooth is not so keen,
> Because thou art not seen,
>   Although thy breath be rude.
>
> Freeze, freeze, thou bitter sky,
> That dost not bite so nigh
>   As benefits forgot;
> Though thou the waters warp,
> Thy sting is not so sharp
>   As friend remember'd not.

These lines are from "Aurora Leigh," Mrs. Browning; they are an example of the slow parenthesis:

Of writing many books there is no end,
And I, who have written much in prose and verse,
For others' uses, will write now for mine,—
Will write my story for my better self
(As when you paint your portrait for a friend,
Who keeps it in a drawer, and looks at it
Long after he has ceased to love you, just
To hold together what he was and is),
Will I, etc., etc.

The next gives us an example of transfer in emphasis:

A lean cheek, which you have *not;* a blue eye and sunken, *which* (you have not); an unquestionable spirit, which *you* have not; a beard neglected, which you *have* not:—but I pardon you for *that;* for simply your having in beard is a younger brother's revenue:—then your hose should be ungartered, your bonnet unbanded, your sleeve unbuttoned, your shoe untied, and everything about you demonstrating a careless desolation. But you are no such man, you are rather [point-device] in your acoutrements, as loving yourself, than being the lover of any other!

A clause unemphatic through repetition:

"The worst is not,
So long as we can say—This is the worst."

Transfer in emphasis:

"But yet!
I do not *like* but yet, it does allay

>   The good *precedence; fie* upon but yet;
>   But yet is a *gaoler* to bring forth
>   Some monstrous *malefactor*."

Contrast:

> " Admire, exult, despise, laugh, weep, for here
>   There is such matter for all feeling :—Man !
>   Thou pendulum betwixt a smile and tear."

Psychological positives and negatives:

> "How poor, how rich, how abject, how august,
> How complicate, how wonderful is man !
> How passing wonder He who made him such !
> Who centered in our make such strange extreme,
> From different natures marvellously mixt,
> Connexion exquisite of distant worlds !
> Distinguish'd link in Beauty's endless chain !
> Midway from nothing to the Deity !
> A beam ethereal, sullied, and absorbed ;
> Though sullied and dishonoured, still divine !
> Dim miniature of greatness absolute !
> An heir of glory ! a frail child of dust !
> Helpless immortal ! Insect infinite !
> A worm ! a god !

www.ingramcontent.com/pod-product-compliance
Lightning Source LLC
Chambersburg PA
CBHW020857230426
43666CB00008B/1216